The Church at the Turning Points of History

BY

GODFREY KURTH

SIXTH THOUSAND
AUTHORIZED TRANSLATION FROM THE FIFTH
FRENCH EDITION BY
RT. REV. MONSIGNOR VICTOR DAY
Vicar General of Helena
REVISED AND ANNOTATED EDITION

NAEGELE PRINTING CO., HELENA, MONT.

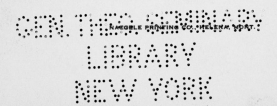

Nihil Obstat

Joseph C. Willging.

Censor Ex-Officio.

Imprimatur

+ Joannes Patritius Carroll

Episcopus Helenensis.

In Nativitate Domini
Helenae, Montanae, A. D. 1924.

FOREWORD.

The mission of the Church is to all nations and to all ages. "Going therefore, teach ye all nations . . . . . Teaching them to observe all things whatsoever I have commanded you; and behold, I am with you all days, even to the consummation of the world". The doctrines of the Church must be always and everywhere the same, namely those her Divine Founder commanded her to preach. To teach them effectively, however, she must sympathize with the manners, customs and institutions of the various peoples she meets in her pathway across the centuries, adapting herself to their genius, to their forms of government and civilization. Like the Apostle, she must "become all things to all men, that she may save all". Hence, she has been obliged in the course of her history to break with old systems and organizations with which her life had become interwoven, in order to conform to new conditions of human society. This was not an easy thing to do. It always entailed a struggle. It often meant a crisis in her work of evangelization. If she were a mere human institution, she could not, any

more than the other human institutions whose
wrecks strew the highway of history, have
survived the onslaughts that have been made
upon her. That she has passed every crisis
and triumphantly outridden every storm that
has beaten upon her for nearly two thousand
years is evidence of the divinity of her mission
to the nations and to the ages.

Her first struggle was with the judaizing
influences which surrounded her cradle.
Jewish thought and sentiment and practices
threatened to restrict her work to the Jews
and to those who would be willing to accept
Jewish religious traditions and customs. In
the Council of Jerusalem she took the bold
step that enabled her to break away from her
Jewish moorings and take to the high seas of
the Gentile world—to encounter storms and
tempests, but also enclose in her net the
copious draught of fishes. From that time
forward she emphasized the universal character of her mission, and, in the language of
the Apostle, became a debtor to Gentile and
Jew alike.

Again, when she had converted the Gentile
world and ruled humanity from the very
capital of civilization, there was danger that
her destinies had become irrevocably linked
with those of the Roman Empire. Hence,
when the Barbarian invasions had sounded
the knell of Roman civilization, many thought
the Church would disappear in the great

cataclysm. But true to her universal mission, she offered the message of salvation to the Barbarians. These accepted the cross and carried it, together with the Christian civilization of which it is the symbol, to the remotest corners of the old Roman world.

The converted Barbarians in the gratitude of their hearts lavished upon the Church the wealth they had amassed, and Barbarian kings shared with her bishops and priests their own temporal rulership over the people. The prestige and power thus given to the Church became in time a real menace to her. In exchange for it kings persuaded themselves, contrary to the canons of the Church, that they had a right to select candidates for vacant sees and abbacies. The kings of Germany even went so far as to arrogate to themselves the nomination of the Sovereign Pontiff, and for a period of about one hundred years no Pope could ascend the chair of Peter without their approbation or consent. Under such a system royal favor and willingness to do the bidding of the king, rather than priestly virtue, became the chief qualifications for ecclesiastical dignities. The result was that simony and a general laxity of morals grew apace among the clergy, and heresy began to make inroads upon the people. The Church was stripped of her independence in things spiritual and became a mere creature of the State. Feudalism had, indeed, en-

riched her, but it was at the price of chains
and slavery.

The evil was grave beyond all precedent.
It seemed irremediable, because it had taken
hold of the vitals of the Church; it attacked
the very source of her life. And yet, with the
vitality guaranteed to her by divine promise,
her great heart slowly drove out from her almost atrophied body the fatal infection and
clothed it again with health and liberty. The
fire of Christian and priestly life which, in
the monasteries at least, had not wholly died
out, was fanned into a flame; Pope Leo IX
and his two successors, by taking possession
of the Pontifical See only after the prescriptions of the canon law had been complied
with, prepared the way for the constitution of
Nicholas II on the election of Sovereign
Pontiffs; and the open warfare of Gregory
VII, the immortal Hildebrand, on the right
of Lay Investiture triumphed in the Concordat of Worms, the State giving back to the
Church complete freedom in all canonical
elections, from that of the Pope down to those
of the lowest ecclesiastical dignitaries.

This was the greatest triumph of the
Church. Free from the embrace of Feudalism, she extinguished heresy, united all
Europe in defence of the Holy Sepulcher,
brought Gothic art to its highest perfection,
created and developed the great universities,
placed saints upon the thrones of kings, be-

came the supreme authority of the West and the spiritual oracle of the world.

Independent in her own spiritual domain, the Church had succeeded in uniting all the states of Europe in one grand Christian republic, of which the Pope was the acknowledged spiritual chieftain. In the quarrels of kings with one another or with their subjects, the Pope was the supreme arbitrator. His decisions were final, because they had back of them the moral sanction which the common acceptance of Christian principles made effective. This happy condition was not to last. The spirit of nationalism, jealous of whatever savored of foreign interference, fostered by a laicizing movement envious of the social prestige of the clergy and directed by a general infatuation for Roman law, gradually developed a condition favorable to royal absolutism. The death of Pope Boniface VIII and the triumph of Philip the Fair widened the breach between the Church and the State, and hastened the day when kings everywhere would proclaim political maxims to be independent of religious belief and absolve themselves from conformity to the principles of Christian morality in the conduct of their realms—hastened the day when national policy would be no longer regulated by the moral standard which Christianity had set up for the individual—the day when monarchs, disregarding the ecumenical character

of the Church of Christ, would establish state
religions of their own making. It was the old
autocracy of the Roman Caesars, who arrogated to themselves the title of king and
pontiff, brought back again to earth—an
autocracy which Christianity had banished
from the world. The Church could only protest and, sitting at the foot of the cross, await
the return of better days.

Since kings refused the moral guidance of
the Church and became a law unto themselves,
it was only natural that the influence of the
Church in securing obedience to the royal
authority was weakened. The bad example of
the kings had its effect upon their subjects.
The Church had, indeed, captured the Renaissance and made it issue in that grand
efflorescence of Christian art and architecture, of poetry and music, of painting and
sculpture, which will never cease to command
the admiration of the world. But the by-
products of the Renaissance were free thought
and licentiousness. These were fashioned into
a system under the direction of Voltaire and
Rousseau and accepted by the French cultured classes as the ideal of political society.
The rapid translation of the ideal into the
real, as is the custom in France, resulted in
the French Revolution. The rule of force,
which kings were obliged to substitute for the
discredited moral sanction of the Church, had
reacted against themselves.

That the French Revolution swept away the altar as well as the throne is not surprising when we consider that the intellectual and moral distemper referred to above had for a long time been working in the bosom of the nation—that for nearly five hundred years the Church had been excluded from the political councils of the country and deprived of the vitalizing power that comes from the fearless and open profession of the doctrine of the supreme headship of the Sovereign Pontiff— that the clergy belonged to a privileged order and were thus held responsible before the bar of public opinion for the mistakes of the regime of which they were supposed to form a part—that prelates and priests, notwithstanding the irreproachable private lives of the vast majority of them, lacked intellectual courage and without protest accepted the humiliation of the Church. In a word, the Church was not properly represented in France during the perilous times which begot the Revolution. If she had been there in the full vigor of her apostolate, either the monarchy would have been shorn of its autocratic power, or the forces of the Revolution would have been directed along the lines of Christian teachings—as were those of the American Revolution, thanks in no small measure to the wisdom and prudence, to the enlightened zeal and fearless public spiritedness of America's first Bishop.

But the failure of the Church was only local and temporary. If she slept during the days of the French Revolution, it was like the sleep of Jesus in the tempest-tossed bark of Peter. To some her awakening may seem tardy, but it is an awakening as fruitful as was that of the Master. Her voice is potent today throughout the world against the winds and the waves of anarchy and despotism that threaten to engulf human society. Her great Pontiff, Leo XIII, in immortal encyclicals, which have become the textbook of statesmen the world over, has proclaimed the Christian constitution of states and the Magna Charta of the laboringman's liberties. And Benedict XV is heard above the roar of battle urging the warring nations to respect the old principles of Christian morality as the only means of mitigating the horrors of war and of securing a just and lasting peace.

The present world-war is sure to issue in the universal acceptance of democracy. And he must be blind to the lessons of history who does not see that the Catholic Church—because of her universality, because of her wonderful organization, because of her adaptability to the genius of every people, because of her superiority to all merely temporal interests, because of her spiritual triumphs throughout the centuries, because of the divine authority with which she speaks—is the one great moral power remaining in the world which can breathe into democracy that spirit of justice and liberty which alone will insure its permanency and make its reign a blessing to humanity.

* * * * * * * * *

Such are the considerations which Godefroid Kurth puts before us in his book, entitled "The Church at the Turning Points of History". It is enough to say in praise of this eminent professor of history in the University of Liége that his writings have been crowned by several European Academies. That the book now appears for the first time in an English dress is due to the painstaking care of Right Reverend Victor Day, Vicar General of the Diocese of Helena. The vigor of thought and language of the original French is maintained in the translation. To those who desire a comprehensive view of the great crises in the history of Christian civilization we cheerfully recommend this really great work.

✠ *John P. Carroll,*

Bishop of Helena

February 22, 1918.

GODFREY KURTH

A WORD TO THE READER

"The Catholic Encyclopedia and Its Makers" gives the following biographical sketch of the Author of "L'Eglise aux Tournants de l'Histoire" (The Church at the Turning Points of History):

Godfrey Kurth, C. S. G., born at Arlon, Belgium, May 11, 1847; died at Assche, Brabant, January 4, 1916. Professor at the State University of Liége, Belgium, 1872-1906; director Belgian Historical Institute, Rome, 1906-1916. Secretary Royal Historical Commission; member of: The Academy of the Catholic Religion (Rome); the Royal Society of Literature (London); the Society for Rhenish Historical Research (Cologne); The Dutch Literary Society (Leyden); the Madrid Historical Academy; the Academy of Belles Lettres (Barcelona); Royal Academy of Belgium; hon. member of the National Academy (Rheims); titular member of the Royal Academy of Conchology; president of the Board of Administration of the Royal Library; doctor honoris causa of the Catholic University (Louvain); Commander of the Order of Leopold; Knight of the Order of Pius IX. Author of: "Caton l'ancien"; "Etude critique sur Saint-Lambert et son premier biographe"; "La loi de Beaumont en Belgique"; Les Origines de la civilisation moderne" (6 eds.); "Les Origines de la ville de Liége"; "Histoire poétique des Mérovingiens"; "La frontière linguistique en Belgique et dans le nord de la France", 2 vols.; "Ste Clotilde" (10 eds.); "Les études franques"; "L'église aux tournants de l'histoire" (5 eds.); "Clovis", 2 vols. (2 eds.); "Saint-Boniface" (4 eds.); "Chartes de l'Abbaye de Saint-Hubert en Ardenne"; "Notger de Liége et la civilisation au Xe siècle", 2 vols.; "La cité de Liége au moyen âge", 3 vols.; "Manuel de l' histoire de Belgique" (3 eds.) ¡ "Abrégé de l'histoire de Belgique" (2 eds.); "Manuel d'histoire universelle", 2 vols.; "Notre nom national"; "Mizraim, Souvenirs d' Egypte"; "La nationalité Belge"; founder and first director of "Archives Belges, revue critique d'historiographie nationale". The Catholic Encyclopedia contains the following articles from his pen: Belgium; Burgundy; Charles Martel; Clotilda, Saint; Clovis; Egmont, Count of Lamoral; Frankenburg, Johann Heinrich, Graf von; Franks; Fredegarius; Granvelle, Antoine Perrenot de; Netherlands; Philip II (Spain).

The reader owes the above sketch to the courtesy of the Encyclopedia Press.

Should "The Church at the Turning Points of History" prove acceptable to the reading public, it might be followed by a translation of Godfrey Kurth's unique and remarkable work: "Les Origines de la Civilisation Moderne".

Brief historical notes are occasionally given to enable the person who has not recently studied general history to read the lectures of the master-historian, Godfrey Kurth, with more pleasure and profit.

Gratitude compels me to acknowledge my indebtedness to the Reverend Stephen J. Sullivan, D. D. for his valuable assistance in the translation of the present work.

Victor Day

PREFACE OF THE AUTHOR

This booklet contains the substance of a course of lectures given at the "Women's University Extension" in Antwerp, during the scholastic year 1897-1898.

This explains sufficiently the plan and style of the work. There was question of presenting to an intelligent audience the great lines of a tableau which must be surveyed at one glance, if one wishes to grasp its vast and striking unity.

Friendly critics have asked me to give references for the statements made. I have not deemed it wise to burden with annotations lectures which aim to present ideas rather than to state facts. As will be seen, I take it for granted that the latter are known to the reader, and I trust that he will take my word for occasional statements of facts with which he may not be familiar.

GODFREY KURTH

General Analytical Index

The Mission of the Church

The Church and the Jews

The Church and the Barbarians

The Church and Feudalism

The Church and Neo-Caesarism

The Church and the Renaissance

The Church and the Revolution

The Mission of the Church

In the history of mankind considered as a whole, there are two grand divisions. On the one hand, there is the ancient world seated in the darkness of death; on the other hand, the modern world which advances in the light of the Gospel. This is, beyond compare, the greatest fact of history.

Christianity opens new era for humanity.

The opposition between these two worlds is sharp and well-defined. The line of demarcation which separates them is very clearly drawn. It is not an imperceptible and gradual evolution that leads humanity from the one to the other. It is rather a new spiritual influence, a mighty impulse which brings about an immediate and radical change. We know the precise date of this great change, and we have taken that date as the starting point of our chronology. It is the Christian era that opens the annals of a new creation and a new humanity.

What is the vital principle of this new creation? It is the new ideal brought into the world by Jesus Christ, or, to adhere to the

simplicity of the Gospel language, it is what
Jesus Christ Himself calls the New Law.
Deposited within the bosom of humanity as
leaven in the paste—this comparison is also
His—it produces there the marvelous fermentation that transforms the most refractory elements. Allow this leaven to do its work. The
more it acts, the more substantial and nour-
ishing will be the bread of civilization.

Christianity offers supreme happiness to all.

The principle of Christian civilization is
essentially opposed to that of ancient society.
Compare the two worlds: on the surface you
perceive many characteristics common to
both, but at the bottom of these common
traits you perceive the irreducible contradiction of the fundamental idea on which they
are based. There is question not merely of
a difference of degree, but of a difference of
nature which has a bearing on a most important matter, on the most vital interests
of humanity. The two societies differ in
their respective conception of life and the
solution they give to the problem of existence.
Antiquity has never proposed this problem
in formal terms; moreover the ancients lacked
both the courage and the knowledge required
to solve it. In practice, however, they
have always given the wrong solution. Christianity has proposed the question boldly and
has answered it in a triumphant manner.

Why was man placed in this world, and what is the end of his existence here below? Must he be only the ephemeral specta- tor of the tableau of creation, or the unconsci- ous instrument of some mission higher than his own, or the lamentable plaything of blind forces that dispute the possession of his senses and of his heart? Is he, with the contradic- tions that are at the root of his being, and with his boundless aptitude for suffering, the abortive child of this world and the play- thing of an eternal illusion? Has he a future to conquer, an end to attain, and are this future and this end worth the effort they cost him? Or is he only a fortuitous and lamentable combination of elements associated for the time in a community of joys and of sufferings, to be finally disassociated and recomposed later on in the eternal circle of pitiless fatalities?

Christianity answers these questions with absolute clearness and certitude.

Man is not a child of chance—he is the creature of God. God has made him the king of creation. He has given him a mind to know Him, a heart to love Him, and a will to be in accord with His own. He has opened before him the way he must follow, He has taught him the law he must observe, He has promised him eternal happiness as the reward for fidelity in serving Him. In other words, He has made the fidelity of man to the Supreme Being the condition of his supreme happiness.

Paganism brings empty pleasure to few.

This is the teaching of Christianity. In this promise all religions and philosophies join Christianity. But, unable to rise with her to the pure and high sources whence flows the true happiness of the human race, they flutter about with their short wings in a common and feverish aspiration for happiness. They also promise happiness to men, but they do not understand it as Christianity does. The good in which they make men hope to find this happiness, has none of the qualities that give it stability. It is not absolute, it is not pure, it is not eternal. It is a sum of joys that do not go beyond the duration of time, the boundaries of earth, or the reach of mankind. In a word, it is not happiness, but pleasure; sometimes pleasure of a higher order, when, as with elevated souls, it consists in the intoxication of glory; other times pleasure of a low and degrading kind, when, as with the multitude, it limits itself to the gross pleasures of the senses. In every case, whether it be intellectual or material, it is but the shadow, or to speak better, it is only the appearance of happiness. And yet this sort of pleasure—and this alone—antiquity had the courage to promise to men, and the power to procure for some of them. And antiquity never meant anything else when there was mention of *Roman felicity,* that fiction so dear to the statesmen of the Empire of the Caesars.

Quite a complicated machinery was needed to realize this paltry happiness. It was necessary to place in common the powers of all men, and to deposit them in the hands of a being produced by their collectivity, the State. Invested with all the power and the rights which before could have resided in all and in each of its members, the State undertook to procure for them the sum of all the enjoyments which constituted their ideal of happiness. These enjoyments may be summed up in two words: idleness and voluptuousness. To eat one's bread without labor and to pass one's time in amusement was, to use a familiar and at the same time a very exact phrase, the *maximum* of felicity as the ancient State understood it.

It was not much, and, nevertheless, how few could enjoy this meager happiness. It could be the lot of but a small minority. If a man lives without work, he forces others to work for him; if he lives for pleasure, it is necessary for him to have an army of people who will furnish him amusement. There existed, therefore, legions of slaves of every kind to procure bread and pleasure for the favorites of the State; the terrestrial paradise of the chosen few had for its correlative

the terrestrial hell of the multitude. Even
at this price, were the elect sure of their happiness? No: they wasted away with disgust
and weariness. For, such is the inexorable
providential law attached to the abuse of
earthly pleasures. Pleasure, chosen as an
end, is a cruel god who devours his adorers.
In the midst of pleasure, the happy ones of
the world felt themselves taken at the throat
by the lurking hand of death which crouched
within their poisoned joys. They saw these
sources of prosperity that formerly were fed
by the sacred sweat of labor dry up around
them. The Empire was no longer defended
except by Barbarians; public works were
carried on only by slaves; the fields,
deserted by the farmer, were fruitless;
the ranks of human society began to
thin out in a dreadful manner. Happiness, as understood by the ancient world,
was nothing but the slow suicide of society.
Thus, universal misery sprang from the very
principle of the civilization that had promised
to its votaries happiness here below.

The happiness Christianity promises to
man, presents a sum of characteristics radically opposed to those of the *Roman felicity*.
It consists in the enjoyment of a Supreme
Being, that is to say, in the union with God.
It is perfect like the Good which is its principle, it is indefectible, it is eternal, it is made
for all on the sole condition that they obey

The Church and the Jews

In this lecture, I shall try to answer this question: How did Christianity become a universal religion? At first sight it would seem that this is not a question at all. At this day it is indeed beyond question that Christianity is, by its nature, the religion of humanity and that, once she had received her mission to preach the Gospel to every creature, she could not shirk it without perishing. But these considerations, which are enough for the faith of the believer, do not satisfy the curiosity of the historian. For, what interests the historian is not merely the terminal of the journey but the course of travel as well. The question under consideration comes then to this: What obstacles hindered Christianity from becoming a universal religion? and how did she succeed in overcoming them?

Christianity hindered in expansion by question of Ancient Law.

The great obstacles, or, rather, the chief danger that the Church encountered in the first years lay in her ignorance of the attitude to be assumed concerning the Ancient Law and Israel. The lapse of time has solved

this problem clearly and with precision, and
now it is within the grasp of a child. There
is nothing now in common between Israel
rejected, shut up within her synagogue, and
the people of God gathered about the Church.
But it was quite different when the Church
came into being. Far from considering Israel
as the people of reprobation, the Christians,
one and all, the Apostles at their head, continued to regard the Jews as the people of
God. Being Jews themselves and holding
fast to the Law of Moses, they saw in Christianity the complement of the Law and in
the Church the consummate flower that came
forth to crown the fertile root of Jesse.

Christian Church Jewish in origin.

And how could they have believed otherwise? For centuries Israel had waited for
the Messias, who was to come according to
the promise of the prophets to establish the
kingdom of God, and to bring upon earth the
reign of justice and peace. It mattered not
whether this kingdom was of a temporal
order—as the greater part of the Jews believed—or of the spiritual order—as the
Christians admitted from the beginning—
this much was certain to them all:—it was to
be the kingdom of Israel. Was it not the
people of Israel who had received the divine
promises? Was it not Abraham to whom it

had been foretold that his posterity would be
as numerous as the stars of heaven, and was it
not David to whom God had announced that
he had made a covenant with his house and
that from him should come forth the Desired
of all Nations? Was not Israel the guardian
of the Law, of that Law which Christ said He
had come to fulfill and not to destroy? And
had He not said further that He had come
first for the wandering sheep of the flock of
Israel, and had He not recommended His
Apostles to preach the Gospel first to the
Jews?

How, then, could the Church have been to
men of that time other than an extension of
Israel, a new budding forth of Jacob? She
was wholly Jewish: her Divine Founder was
a Jew, the apostles and disciples were Jews,
the first converts also were Jews. The three
thousand persons whom Saint Peter baptized
at Jerusalem, on the day of Pentecost, were
Jews *of the dispersion;* and he addressed
Jews exclusively, when he said: "Therefore
let all the house of Israel know most certainly
that God hath made both Lord and Christ,
this same Jesus, whom you have crucified."(*)
And later, when the apostles and disciples
carried the Gospel beyond Judea, they tarried
only in the towns where there were Jews,
stayed in the Jewish quarters, frequented the

* The Acts II, 36.

synagogues, and it was there they announced
to all that the Messias of the prophets had
come and that He was called Jesus of Naza-
reth. In a word, everywhere, throughout the
entire world as at Jerusalem, the Church was
sinking its roots deep into the synagogue,
and the first Christian congregations were in
truth assemblies of Jews.

Gentile converts required to become naturalized Jews.

This does not mean that this Christian
Church of Jewish nationality wished to close
her doors to the gentiles. On the contrary,
she dreamed of gathering within her embrace
all the people of the earth, in order to comply
with the demand of Christ. The Jewish
people themselves never exercised towards the
rest of humankind that absolute isolation
which ill-informed historians impute to them.
At all times they strove to win to
their faith the children of other nations,
and their proselytism was as active as
it was sincere. The Gospel itself gives testimony of this in these words: "Woe to you
scribes and pharisees: because you go round
about the sea and the land to make one prose-
lyte: and when he is made, you make him the
child of hell twofold more than yourselves."

Thus the people of Israel were surrounded
by a throng of proselytes. One class of proselytes were called *Proselytes of the Gate,* because they were permitted to pass only the

first gate of the court of the Temple: they were such as acknowledged the true God, abstained from all idolatry and observed the seven precepts of the natural law. The second class were called *Proselytes of Righteousness,* and were those who accepted the whole Jewish religion and who pledged themselves to observe all the precepts without exception. Initiated through the rite of circumcision, they had the same rights and the same duties as the Israelites by birth.

In general, in order to become servers of the true God, the proselytes were obliged, if I may use a modern expression, to become naturalized Jews:—this was the absolute condition. The Proselytes of Righteousness possessed, in virtue of the rite of circumcision, their final naturalization papers; henceforth they became part not only of the synagogue, but of the Jewish nation. The Proselytes of the Gate, initiated in a manner less complete, saw themselves excluded, by that very fact, from participation in the Jewish worship; the Temple remained closed to them; they were but the protégés and clients of Israel, or, if you like, they were Jews of second rank. In a word, without denying to anyone the right to adore with her the true God, Israel expected each worshiper to receive from her, in some way, the investiture, to become a Jew in more or less measure, according to the right he wished to enjoy. The Jews regarded themselves as forming within the family of the servers of God the central nucleus, the circle of the elite; they meant to be to the rest of humanity what Levi had been within his fold, the race marked forever with a sign of predilection, the priestly tribe which stood as the intermediary between God and man.

Such was the Jewish view-point, which the first Christians, Jews themselves, carried with them into Christianity. They saw in the Church a synagogue of superior order to which God had revealed the obscure meaning of the prophecies, but a synagogue neverthe- less into which no one could enter without be- ing a member either by birth or by adoption of the people of Israel. Now then, I ask, was this really the way to bring nations to em- brace the Gospel, to oblige them to give up their nationality as well as their religion? When one sees even to-day the injury that national susceptibilities, often the best found- ed, cause to the Catholic apostolate and to the advance of the Gospel, it can be surmised what would have been the result if, at that time, there had been imposed upon nations the most unbearable of all humiliations—na- tional renouncement. Allow me to illustrate by an example. If to-day the German Luther- ans, the English Episcopalians, the Russian Schismatics and other peoples whom we de- sire to unite within the unity of faith, were told that, in order to become Catholic, they must first become Frenchmen, do you think it would hasten their conversion and that there would be any hope of seeing them make profession of our faith? And yet France is a great and glorious nation, enjoying the respect of all, even of those who hate her; while the Jews were a little nation universally despised, an object of hatred to the whole human race, as Tacitus states, about whom were spread most repugnant tales. For a Greek or a Roman to renounce his national title and become a Jew would have meant not only to give up his national traditions but also to embrace cheerfully opprobrium and ridicule, by assuming a nationality that was in a way under the ban of civilization.

Christian Church without light on subject.

Here we see how Israel, by her pretensions to leadership in the kingdom of God, hindered the propagation of the Gospel. So long as Israel stood between the Savior and the human race, the human race was bound to keep away from the Savior. This is plain to us of modern times who look at this epoch at the distance necessary for clear vision and who have sufficient freedom of mind to form a fair judgment. But such was not the position of those who, whether Christian or Jew, lived in the midst of occurring events without being able to foresee their course. How could they foresee it without being prophets? And

how would they have dared to choose a line of
conduct without a special revelation? The
apostles themselves were without light upon
this weighty problem. The Gospels did not
furnish them with the solution. They were
children of Israel and they had to be on their
guard lest they should lay themselves open to
calumny; under the conditions, could they
have been other, should they have been other,
than good patriots and faithful observers of
the Law of Moses? And this they were,
all of them. The most finished type of the
true Jew, whom all the Jews venerated and
delighted to call the Just, was himself an
apostle, nay more, he was a relative of Jesus
—known as St. James the Less. Certainly
these are not the sort of men who could guess
the danger that threatened the Church in its
deadly grapple with Judaism, much less break
the bond that seemed to tie the Church forever to the synagogue.

Thus, humanly speaking, Christianity
found itself in its early days in a blind alley.
It remained a national religion, it was not
becoming a universal religion. It was merely
a phenomenon of the inner history of Judaism, a religious revolution that could arouse
only the Jews, and attract to itself only the
scornful curiosity of the rest of the world.
The pagan world would hear only the little
that was said of it by the Roman historians,
Suetonius and Tacitus, namely, that a little

nation which on account of its fanaticism was consigned to the execration of humanity had one day been set in turmoil by innovations preached within its fold by a certain Chrestus and that, in order to end these troubles, the Jews had been expelled from Rome.

Vision of Peter solves problem—Baptism of Cornelius.

It was at this moment that there occurred the extraordinary scene of which the Acts of the Apostles have preserved a detailed account. I ask permission to reproduce this sacred page; none more fateful is found in the history of Christianity.

There was in the city of Caesarea, in Palestine, a centurion of the Roman army, named Cornelius. He was a just man and God-fearing. One day an angel appeared to him saying that his prayers had been agreeable to the Lord, and that he was to send for one Simon Peter who was then living at Joppe, in the house of a tanner by the seaside. Cornelius obeyed and despatched three men to the Apostle. I leave the words to the inspired text:

"And on the next day whilst they were going on their journey, and drawing nigh to the city, Peter went up to the higher parts of the house to pray about the sixth hour.

And being hungry, he was desirous to taste something. And as they were preparing, there came upon him an ecstasy of mind;

And he saw the heavens opened, and a certain vessel descending, as it were a great linen sheet let down by the four corners from heaven to the earth.

Wherein were all manner of fourfooted beasts, and creeping things of the earth, and fowls of the air.

And there came a voice to him: Arise, Peter, kill, and eat.

But Peter said: Far be it from me; for I never did eat anything that is common and unclean.

And the voice spoke to him again the second time: That which God hath cleansed do not thou call common.

And this was done thrice: and presently the vessel was taken up into heaven.

Now whilst Peter was doubting within himself what the vision that he had seen should mean: behold the men who were sent from Cornelius, inquiring for Simon's house, stood at the gate.

And when they had called, they asked, if Simon, who is surnamed Peter, were lodged there?

And as Peter was thinking of the vision, the Spirit said to him: Behold three men seek thee.

Arise, therefore, get thee down, and go with them, doubting nothing: for I have sent them." (*)

---

* Acts, X., 9-20.

Peter, obedient to the Holy Ghost, accompanied the messengers to Caesarea where he baptized Cornelius and his whole family. For the first time there was in the Church a Gentile who had not passed through the synagogue.

The vision of St. Peter is the divine solution of the irritating problem. Under a most expressive symbolic formula the vision announces that the ancient Law is no longer binding on the Christians, and that consequently one can be a Christian without being a Jew. The Church will not be a Jewish community; it will be an international society where shall meet as brothers, without distinction of rite or race, the Jew and the Gentile, the master and the slave, the poor and the rich. In vain then does Israel promise herself the first place in the kingdom of God. Israel can disappear without causing a vacancy; her mission is ended and her place henceforth will be taken by a spiritual Israel made up of all the faithful.

One will understand the excitement that was stirred up in Jerusalem at news of the baptism in Caesarea. St. Peter was interpellated and had to explain; he made known that he had acted only on the order of the Lord, and his contradictors kept silent. As to the faithful, they repeated among themselves:

"God then hath also to the gentiles given repentance unto life."

Ultra-Jewish Christians still object.

Accordingly it might seem that all difficul-
ties had been removed and that all discussion,
all hesitation had ceased in the Church now
that its course had been set right by the hand
of God Himself. But this would be to dis-
regard the intensity of doctrinal feeling.
Those Christians who put their Jewish patriotism above their Christian faith did not give
up their favorite idea concerning the privilege
of Israel. This doctrine was part, so to speak,
of their flesh and blood; it was one of the
constituent elements of their faith, it was
identified in their thoughts with the Christian
doctrine. They seemed to have let the baptism at Caesarea pass as a miraculous exception, not as a rule. Who knows but that more
than one bore a grudge against Peter on
account of his vision, looked on him as a
dreamer and visionary. In any case, heedless
that Peter had spoken, they calmly perse-
vered in their contention that one could not
become a Christian without first becoming
a naturalized Jew.

Such was the situation when one day there
came to Jerusalem news far more serious
than that of the baptism of a single family
of gentiles. It was told that in Antioch, in
that great city which was the queen of the

victim of the fanatics, proclaimed his orthodoxy before the whole Church; he sealed
with him that fraternal union which time has
consecrated into a glorious partnership—making them the household gods of the new Rome.
Not less decisive was the attitude of James
the Just, the most orthodox and pious of the
Jews, on whom all the reactionaries relied, who
spoke in accordance with Peter and threw
the weight of his unequalled prestige in support of the much disparaged innovations.
After the discussion, the First Council flung
open the doors of the Church to the nations
in this sublime declaration: "It hath seemed
good to the Holy Ghost and to us, to lay no
further burden upon you than the necessary
things."

The Council of Jerusalem had saved Christianity, but it had sacrificed Judaism. In de-
ciding that the Church would be Catholic,
that is to say, international, it had killed the
national pretensions of the Jewish clique.
Then ended forever the time-honored dream
in which the seers had seen the children of Israel seated on the very steps of the
throne whence the Messias ruled all the nations of the earth. But it was to be a "spiritual Israel," a symbolic Sion that the prophets had announced; strangers were taking
the place of the children of the family at the
banquet; from the stones by the roadside God
was raising up children to Abraham. Thus

at last the hidden meaning of the Scripture was revealed. More than one Christian Jew must have said to himself that God was not fulfilling the promise made to Abraham and to Jacob, that He was repelling the people with whom He had an everlasting covenant and that He was covering with shame the daughter of Sion. Many of them, like the captive Hebrews at Babylon, sat and wept bitter tears as they remembered disinherited Sion. "Upon the rivers of Babylon, there we sat and wept: when we remembered Sion." Ps., CXXXVI., 1. Let us greet with respect this patriotic grief than which there is scarcely any more exalted, but let us not forget that the cause of the Church was superior to that of Israel, and that the interests of humanity go before those of country. Some of the Christian Jews were not resigned. After the Council of Jerusalem, they continued their desperate opposition to the teachings of the Church, to the definitions that she had promulgated, to the apostolate of the Gentiles. Clinging obstinately to the old national prejudices which they identified with orthodoxy, they soon became but a small refractory sect cast upon the road to heresy. The catastrophe in which Jerusalem perished some years later drowned their opposition in a deluge of blood and was, to the Christian Jews, a decisive revelation which came to confirm that of Joppe. After this it was

plain that Israel was no longer the people of
God, but a rejected nation. It is no
longer worth while to fix upon it the attention
of history.

First turning point in Church's history.

As for the Church, she had just separated
her cause from the precarious destiny of a
nation. She had refused to espouse the cause
of the petty contingencies of history so as not
to fail in her universal mission. Peter's
bark had cut the rope that bound it to
port and was gaining the high seas where,
without doubt, there awaited it storms, but
also miraculous draughts of fishes. Such was
the first turning point in the history of the
modern world.

The Church and the Barbarians

Christianity becomes religion of Roman Empire.

Thenceforth there was nothing to prevent
Christianity from becoming the religion of
the Roman Empire, that is, of all the nations
grouped under the shadow of the Roman
civilization. For indeed what were all the
other dangers awaiting the Church compared
to the danger which had nearly destroyed her
on the threshold of life? The bloody perse-
cutions which marked the three centuries of
her early life proved no obstacle to her growth.
It is true that the fury of her persecutors
spilled the blood of multitudes of her children; but this blood, in accordance with
the expression of an apologist, was a seed of
marvelous fecundity. After three hundred
years of a war of extermination, the Roman
Empire had to acknowledge itself conquered
by its victim and had to surrender to her its
arms. By the edict of Milan, promulgated
in 312, Emperor Constantine the Great proclaimed that henceforth all might adore
God as they wished. This was recognizing
implicitly the right of Christianity to exist.
But it is the glorious privilege of the Catholic
Church that she needs naught but the com-

mon right in order that she may conquer the
universe. As soon as liberty of conscience
was established, the Roman world in its entirety asked for admission into the com-
munion of the faithful, and before the fourth
century had drawn to a close the pagans
saw themselves reduced to the state of a dis-
couraged minority. Christianity had become
the religion of the emperors, the religion of the
provinces; its limits were co-extensive with
those of the Empire. There were Christian
communities on the borders of the Rhine and
of the Danube, as well as on the banks of the
Euphrates and of the Nile; there were Christian communities in Colchis as well as in the
Isle of Britain; and the Christian religion
was sufficiently designated when it was called
the Roman religion.

Christianity linked with Roman civilization.

Thus the humble sect of the Galileans held
the throne of the Caesars and its future was
linked with the destinies of the *eternal civilization*. Truly, the powerful constitution of
the Roman Empire seemed well fitted to last
for all time. Such was the universal belief;
and never did a patriotic dogma rally more
enthusiastic and more sincere adherents than
the creed of all Roman citizens, which found
expression in those proud words: *the eternity
of the Empire!* This formula recurs in the
verses of the poets, in the prayers of the faith-

ful, in the panegyrics of the orators, and even
in the text of the laws. Rome, in the language of its pagan worshipers, was called the
Eternal City, and Christianity, in borrowing
this appellation from the civil language, did
not wish, at least in the beginning, to modify
its traditional sense.

This goes to show that the Christians had
adopted without misgiving the common belief
in the eternity of the Roman civilization.
Whatever the pretensions of their persecutors, the Christians were not less patriotic than
the pagans, though in another way, and their
religious belief contained nothing contrary to
their convictions as citizens. Nay more, they
found in their sacred volumes passages which
seemed to confirm this conviction in a marvelous manner. For what was that fourth
and last empire foretold by Daniel, and compared to iron to symbolize its indestructible
duration, but the Roman Empire? This belief in the eternity of the Roman Empire was,
in a way, part and parcel of their faith; in
fact, it was adduced by the first apologists
as an unanswerable proof of their patriotism.
"How", said one of them, "could we desire
the end of the Empire, since thereby we
would desire the end of the world?"

Barbarians capture Rome.

But dark clouds were gathering slowly on
the horizon, disturbing the serenity of the

world and announcing the catastrophe of the
morrow. The Barbarians, strangers to
Christianity and to civilization, excluded from
the *Roman felicity,* were prowling like wolves
about the sunny domain of the Empire. Rome,
having tried to subdue them, at last came to
the conclusion that its hour for new conquests
was past and that it would never triumph
over them by force of arms. The time came
when the Barbarians were supplying her with
soldiers and it was among them that she recruited her staunchest defenders. Germany
was to antiquity what Switzerland has been
to modern Europe:—a land of lansquenets.
Every year, crossing the Rhine or the Alps,
the warriors of that country came in bands to
hire out the work of their muscular arms to
the generals of the Empire. Lovers of sun-
shine, of wealth, of voluptuousness, they came
in quest of fortune and sometimes they found
the crown. History records the names of
some of these adventurers. One was Maximi-
nus, a type of colossal brute, who under Sep-
timus Severus, ran for hours at a time alongside the chariot of the emperor; later he mur-
dered the Emperor Alexander and usurped
his throne. Another was Odoacer. We meet
him first in history when, on his way to Italy
to sell his services to the Empire, he stopped
at the entrance of the hut of a farfamed and
kindly hermit of Norica, now Bavaria. A
Barbarian of gigantic stature, he had to stoop

to cross the threshold of the hut of the saintly old man whom he wished to greet in passing. A few years later this hireling was king of Italy.

How did the Empire act towards these men whom it could no longer subdue, and of whose services it had incessant need? It concluded that it should rally them to its cause, not by paying them for the blood they would shed for it, but by assimilating them gradually, by making true Romans of them and by handing them over to the Church to make them Christians. This seemed comparatively easy. The Roman civilization was not an exclusive world; it was thrown wide open to any Barbarian who was willing to serve it; and it had sufficient attraction to induce him to exchange his savagery for the Roman life. And in this way, by a sort of tacit agreement, there was worked out the transfusion of the Germanic world into the Roman world:—the former, little by little, took possession of the latter, whilst the latter in turn assimilated the former. It was the peaceful triumph of civilization, superior to all armed conquests. For was it not a triumphant proof of the eternity of the Roman civilization, that a Stilicho (*) and

---

(*) Stilicho, a brave Vandal, shared in the military exploits of Emperor Theodosius (379-395), twice defeated Alaric, king of the Visigoths, and compelled him to abandon Italy. In 405 he conquered the German tribes which had invaded Italy under the leadership of the Ostrogoth Radahais.

an Aetius (1) gained victories in its name,
that a victorious Ataulph (2) proclaimed
the grandeur of Rome in peninent accents,
that Theodoric the Great (3) continued the
work of the Emperors?

In this way the Empire held, towards the
Barbarians, the attitude Israel had maintained towards the Gentiles. Rome could form
no conception of a community of nations save
under the Roman form and with Rome at its
head. Allow me another comparison which
will present my thought in a more striking
manner. The European of to-day cannot
imagine that our modern civilization may
perish; it does not occur to him that one day
the deep masses of Asiatic people or unorgan-
ized hordes of anarchists may destroy it with-

(1) Aetius was the son of an Italian mother and
Gaudentius, a Scythian soldier of the Empire. In the
summer of 450 Aetius, in concert with the brave and loyal
Theodoric, king of the Ostrogoths, relieved Orleans be-
sieged by Attilla, and arrested the progress of the great
Hun on the Catalaunian Fields, near Troyes, where he
won one of the decisive victories of history and saved Europe for Latins, Teutons, Celts and Slavs, against the degraded and odious Huns.

(2) Ataulph, brother and successor to Alaric, chieftain
of the Visigoths, pillaged Rome, but later became reconciled with the Emperor and was commissioned to drive
the Barbarians from Spain. He was assassinated at Barcelona before he had completed his task.

(3) Theodoric the Great, descendant of the royal
Ostrogoth family of the Amali. At eighteen, in 489,
he led a great horde of his countrymen into Italy, where
he destroyed the kingdom of Odoacer in 495 and became
the sole ruler of Italy.

out at the same time unchaining chaos; (*)
such an eventuality would be, in his opinion,
the end of all social life, the return of mankind to the darkness of primeval savagery.
Well then, the Roman of the fourth century
had a view-point very similar—with just this
difference, that, for him, modern civilization
was the Roman Empire.

The Christian Romans see in fall of Rome end of civilization.

Thus, for the second time, the destinies of
the Church were linked with those of a human
institution. Just as the Christian Jews were
firmly convinced that the future of Christianity was indissolubly united with the future
of their own people, so the Christian Romans
imagined that their future was one with the
future of the Empire. The Empire, indeed,
was civilization itself; it was felicity, it was
the perfection of social life, and its chief—in
the solemn language of that day—bore the
title of Prince of the Human Race. Identified with the Empire, the Christian Church,
by that very fact, seemed identified with the
whole human race. She apparently had attained her ideal, with nothing more to ask of

* Since this was written, the events which have taken
place or which are in preparation in the extreme Orient may
have modified the ideas of some. If I mistake not, everyone
is not absolutely convinced of the impossibility of a new
Attila or of a new Genghis Khan, who, equipped with the perfected tools of modern warfare, might throw upon the Western World five hundred million men of the yellow race.
—G. K.

future centuries, and it seemed that it should
be her chief concern to preserve the prevailing
conditions.

Bearing in mind this universal view-point
of the Romans, we may imagine their feelings
as the trend of events, instead of pointing to
the fulfillment of their dreams, seemed,
on the contrary, to foreshadow the destruction
of the Empire by the Barbarians. Every day
they saw increase the number of these hire-
lings who became their plague. Of gigantic
stature, powerful of limb, untidy, red-haired,
with unkempt beard, their legs covered with
rags, ill-smelling, and, moreover, coarse, brutal,
ignorant, talking a hoarse and unintel-
ligible jargon, they spread everywhere, treated the Provinces as their own possession, disregarding wholly the Roman mode of living,
taking from it only its pleasures, for the rest
holding to their own ways without any intention of change. A day indeed came—a day
of shame and of mourning such as the world
had never known—when the savage hordes
captured the Eternal City. Then was the
sanctuary of civilization violated in a most
sacrilegious manner; and men had a forestate
of the end of all things!

And indeed to them the end of the Roman
civilization was the end of the world. If all
that is beautiful in life—style, wealth, well-
being, public games, literature, arts, refined
social manners—was to be suppressed; and if

a flood of barbarism was to be let loose upon a world, radiant, charming, thrilling with the joy of life, would it not mean death to the human race itself? Thus they all said and felt. For to admit for a single moment that the human race could get along without the Roman civilization, and that the future of the former was not indissolubly connected with the prosperity of the latter, was an absurd and impossible thought which no one entertained.

Accordingly, when undeniable signs announced to them the fall of that civilization, the true Romans could but desire death. Some wished to fall in a last intoxication at the banquet of civilization, crowned with roses and drunk with wine; others, wrapped in the folds of the old Roman flag, awaited the fatal blow with stoic despair, even as the senators of yore, seated in their curule chairs, awaited the arrival of the Gallic conqueror. All perished with their ideal, incapable of conceiving any other, witnessing the crash of heaven and of their gods. There are no more tragic sorrows than these, because they touch humanity in those things which it loves and admires the most. All realities may fail so long as the ideal stands; if the ideal also proves false, not only is the heart broken, but the mind is shattered, and the intellect casts itself headlong into nothingness with a cry of utter despair.

In similar crises it is with a fresh outburst
of fanaticism that the vanquished meet the
sentence of destiny. This was particularly
the case with the Romans of Britain. Lo-
cated at the border of the civilized world and
abandoned by Rome at an early hour, they
saw the Anglo-Saxon invasion spread gradually, pushing them back from day to day towards the West, crushing civilization in the
portions of the country they had invaded, and
choking it in the rest of the land. Entrenched
in their fierce patriotism, no longer under-
standing anything of the progress of the
world, they could but protest. Christians
themselves, they were not willing that their
conquerors should be called to the blessings
of the Gospel, and their priests refused to
communicate to the newcomers the light of
the Gospel, unwilling as they were to admit
that one could be both Christian and Anglo-
Saxon, just as the Jews had been unwilling
that one should be Christian and uncircum-
cised. They did not realize that in converting
their conquerors they would save themselves;
they preferred to perish whilst hating them,
rather than to live reconciled with them. It
is the eternal cry of fanaticism:—'rather Turk
than Papist'. The Armenians of to-day realize the significance of such a wish.

Catholic Church sees in Barbarian movement birth of
new civilization.

If the Catholic Church had not understood

her role better than the Briton clergy, if she
had not risen above the resentments of blind
patriotism, Christianity would not have survived, but would have sunk into the abyss
along with the Roman Empire.   But the
Church had a steadier eye and a calmer mind;
she did not despair of humanity, she did not
believe that all was lost because Rome was
doomed.   She viewed the gigantic movement
as a whole, and discovered in it the birth of
a world as yet unknown.   She foresaw the
sublime novelty which then could have been
expressed only by a monstrous coupling of
words, *the Barbarian civilization,* that is, a
civilization that could get on without Rome,
and which would go farther than Rome.   And,
undaunted, conscious of her eternal mission,
she went to those who were then the heralds
of destiny, and, her hand in theirs, she took
the road of the future.

   I have explained elsewhere the genesis of
the movement which was to draw the Catholic
Church in this dirction:—this movement is
identified with the name of the greatest Doctor of the Latin Church, St. Augustine. (*)
Let it suffice to state here that this movement,
conceived in the thought of a man of genius
and nurtured by his disciples, found, from
the end of the fifth century, laborers who carried it from the purely intellectual domain

---

* See Author's Introduction to Clovis, 2 edit. vol. I,
p. XXV.

into that of historical realities. On the one hand, the Gallic episcopacy represented by men like St. Remigius of Rheims and St. Avitus of Vienne, sincerely adherent to the domination of the Barbarians, asked them only to become Christians, and thus bravely renounced the chimerical dream of continuing the Roman civilization. On the other hand, the Papacy, in the person of the greatest man of the sixth century, St. Gregory the Great, took the initiative in the conversion of the Anglo-Saxons, thus fulfilling, from his palace in Rome, the task which the Celtic Church of Britain had disdained to assume. Everywhere, without imposing conditions, the Catholic Church unlocked the gates of her sanctuaries and opened the road of salvation to the new nations. Thus is explained her prodigious success during the sixth century with all the Barbarians, whether Arian (*) or pagan. When these became convinced that they could carry the sweet yoke of Christ without submitting to the heavy yoke of Rome, their prejudices against the Catholic Faith fell to the ground, and its natural superiority over heresy, as well as over paganism, found no longer any obstacle. Joyfully the Barbarian world, whole

---

* The Arians were followers of Arius, a priest of Alexandria in Egypt, who denied the divinity of Christ. Arianism spread far and wide. Arian kingdoms arose in Spain, Africa, Italy. Arianism was condemned at the Council at Nicaea, near Constantinople, in 325 and became extinguished before the eighth century.

and entire, entered into the Church. The peoples became converted as a whole. In less than three centuries all the Germanic nations were won over to Catholicism. More time had been required to convert the Empire, notwithstanding the enormously superior advantages it offered to the apostolate.

The second turning point in Church's history.

We have now passed the second turning point of history, which was inaugurated by the baptism of Clovis. (1) This baptism has often been compared to that of Constantine. (2) I would say that it matches, in a remarkable way, the baptism of the centurion Cornelius. Then, the Church, separating her cause from that of the people of Israel, had gone to the nations and had received them into the Christian community without imposing upon them the obligations of the Judaic Law. This time,

(1) Clovis, (466-511), the founder of the Merovingian line of Frankish kings, married the Christian princess Clotilda in 493, defeated the Alemanni in 496. He was baptized by Saint Remigius the same year in fulfillment of a vow made in battle to the God of Clotilda. As in the case of Constantine the Great the baptism of Clovis led to a rapid diffusion of the Christian religion among his subjects.

(2) Constantine the Great, son of Constantine Chlorus joint-emperor with Galerius, in 312 marched upon Maxentius, the worthless ruler of Rome, and defeated him in the battle of the Milvian Bridge. Before this battle, according to the testimony of Constantine, as recorded by Eusebius a contemporaneous historian, a fiery cross appeared in the sky with this inscription: "In touto nika.' ("In this sign conquer.") Constantine publicly ascribed the victory to the God of the Christians and was the first Roman Emperor to receive Christian baptism.

detaching her destinies from those of the Empire, she went to the Barbarians and put into their hands the scepter of the world without requiring them to wear the dress of the Roman civilization. On both occasions, it was a stroke of strategy of the same superior order. On both occasions, Christianity, the common patrimony of all humanity, had escaped utter destruction. Instead of weeping on the graves of extinct civilizations, Christianity had busied herself with winning to the faith of Christ the nascent communities. She had thus indicated in a precise and explicit manner, and for all centuries to come, that, as she is created to spread the kingdom of God on earth, she cannot identify herself with any of those ephemeral things which are called dynasty, nation, social class, civilization. Having become the universal religion at this price, it is at this price also that she will remain such and continue to make a reality of that sublime epithet given to the Messiah: *the Father of the world to come.*

The Church and Feudalism

Letting the dead bury their dead, letting crumble behind her the moldering edifice of Roman civilization, the Catholic Church, true to her mission, went to the Barbarians and confided to them her destiny. Established in their midst, she chose from them co-laborers, such as St. Boniface (1), Charlemagne (2),

---

(1) St. Boniface, Apostle of Germany, Benedictine Monk, was born in England, May 15, 719. Pope Gregory II gave him full authority to preach the Gospel to the heathens in Germany to the right of the Rhine. When he saw the great results of his labors, he returned to Rome in 722, and was consecrated bishop. Ten years later he was appointed Archbishop with authority to set up bishoprics among the peoples he converted. He drew up a code of laws for the government of the Church in the country. When he had finished his work in Germany he undertook to evangelize the Frisians by whom he was martyred.

(2) Charlemagne (742-814), Emperor of the West and King of the West Franks, was a great patron of letters. Under his reign, notwithstanding continual wars, he established schools throughout his empire. He invited from England Alcuin (A. D. 804), a distinguished scholar and pupil of the Venerable Bede, under whose direction academies were established. The sons of the more wealthy flocked to his lectures. Alcuin spoke Latin, Greek and Hebrew, was master of philosophy. theology. history and mathematics. Under his direction the schools of the Empire became celebrated and scholars from all Europe came to learn wisdom at his feet. The impulse thus given to letters by Charlemagne was continued by his successors. The statues of Constantine the Great and Charlemagne grace the vestibule of St. Peter's in Rome.

Alfred the Great (1), and from the very
first set herself to the task of bringing forth
a new world.

It was a gigantic project, a work of centuries. It would be inspiring and profitable
to consider the undertaking in detail; but
this is not the place to trace a sketch of it—
that I have done elsewhere. (2) My aim
is rather to show how, in the course of her
work, the Church was in danger of falling
victim to the Barbarian she sought to civilize,
and how she finally succeeded in her task.

Generosity of Barbarians to Church.

One must realize what kind of men were
these new peoples, who had just bowed their
heads under the waters of baptism, in the
first centuries of the Middle Ages. With the
exception of a few chosen ones, they were still
only on the threshold of Christianity and,
though baptized, were far from being civilized. They sincerely loved the Christian religion, but their love for it was often crude
and sordid. In their eyes, there were two
ways for a disciple of Christ to give proof of
his faith: to deal vigorous blows to its ene-

---

(1) Alfred the Great (A. D. 849-899), king of the West
Saxons in England. He freed the country of the Danish
invaders, codified and promulgatel laws, founded monasteries, brought learned men from other lands, gave proof
of his own learning by translating several important works
into Anglo-Saxon.

(2) See Author's "Origines de la Civilisation Moderne,"
6th edition. The translator of these pages is at present (in
1924), engaged in putting into an English dress this the
favorite work of Godfrey Kurth.

mies, and to make large benefactions to its
poor. It was their belief—as it is ours—that
charity covers a multitude of sins. And as
they had many sins to be forgiven, they
showed themselves very generous towards the
Church. Nothing more meritorious. The
Church was the mother and the nurse of the
poor. To give to her was not only to contribute to the maintenance of worship and to
the needs of the active ministry, it was to assure the budget of charity and of public in-
struction of which the Church had the sole
charge. Behold how, "for the salvation
of their souls and for the remission of
their sins," as they loved to state in
their acts of donation, the men of that time
were pleased to endow religious institutions
or to found new ones. There was not a mon-
astery, there was not a cathedral or collegiate
church which had not received largesses at
their hands and which they had not made, in
a short time, owner of valuable property, invested with all the social prestige which
rich estates gave in those days. More than
one of these establishments became in this
manner a real power, especially from the days
when kings, outdoing the nobles in their liberality, actually divided their authority with
the Church and granted her in fief entire
counties, with all the political and civil rights,
and made her prelates temporal princes, the
first personages of the state after themselves.

Europe became covered with ecclesiastical principalities, veritable buttresses of the thrones which had created them.

Secular interference with Church affairs.

But so much wealth and prestige, far from being a real power, became on the contrary a supreme danger to the Church. I do not speak here of the violences pure and simple of the depredators, which were, after all, incontestable crimes against right and public order. There is question of a more universal and deeper evil. At once opulent and unarmed, the Church was obliged to confide to lay hands the sword which the State had given her; and because she lacked an hereditary dynasty she was subject to all kinds of rivalry whenever a benefice became vacant. Thus the Church very soon became the plaything of the ambitious and the prey of rival factions. Even those who, in their hours of recollection or repentance, had shown themselves the most generous towards her, did not hesitate to dispose of her dignities, persuading themselves that the liberalities they had bestowed upon her gave them a right of tutelage or protectorate over her. All the great ones were on the watch at the deathbeds of bishops or abbots to contend for the vacant inheritance. Having cadets to place and not wishing to endow them with their own possessions, lest they should reduce the

share of the eldest son, they conceived the
idea of putting the burden of their support
on the shoulders of the Church, by making
them bishops or abbots. The ecclesiastical
hierarchy thus became a dumping ground
for numerous families and the Church became, in a way, an institution of employment
for the cadets of good families.

On the other hand it was to the interest of
kings that ecclesiastical dignities should be
given only to reliable and faithful persons.
In feudal society the political influence acquired by dioceses and monasteries was too
important to leave kings indifferent to
the recruitment of the hierarchy. Again
these rich grants were for them excel-
lent means of government, which they
used to reward the fidelity of some, to
stimulate the zeal of others. They were
not slow, then, contrary to the canons of
the Church, in acquiring almost everywhere
the habit of personally selecting the titularies
of the principal ecclesiastical dignities in
their kingdom. The kings of Germany did
more: they arrogated to themselves, towards
the middle of the tenth century, the nomination of the Sovereign Pontiffs, so that during
about a hundred years (963-1073) no pope
could ascend the see of Peter who had not
been designated or at least agreed on by them.

We should inspect this regime at close
range. When a bishop died, his chapter at

once took possession of the insignia of his priestly dignity:—the ring, which represents his marriage to his diocese, and the crosier, which is the symbol of his authority over his flock, and sent them to the king! But no matter how the messengers hastened on their errand, they were preceded by other travelers quicker than themselves; these were the ambitious ones who dreamed of settling in the vacant chair and who had hurried to the royal court to plead their cause. This was the *steeple-chase* of candidates for the episcopacy. I leave it to the reader to imagine the numberless intrigues, wire-pullings, solicitations, promises, enticing offers made to the more influential courtiers, the selling of influence to the highest bidder, the extraordinary interventions which took place. All this scheming was kept up until they learned that the monarch had made his selection. The lucky candidate was then sent for, and, in a distinctively feudal ceremony, received at the hands of the king the crosier and the ring. There was no longer anything canonical in the whole procedure, there was no longer anything ecclesiastical in the ceremony; the investiture, that is to say, the act by which the new bishop was supposed to be endowed with his powers, was exclusively a lay ceremony.

Lay investiture.

Bear in mind this word *lay investiture*—it

was to become famous in history; it was to be the watchword of the regime. And, meanwhile, note also the character of the relations which henceforth were to exist between Church and State. The great evangelical principle of the distinction of the powers, which is the cornerstone of modern civilization, was violated in the most flagrant manner. The spiritual and temporal were confounded. No longer was there rendered to God what belonged to God. It would seem that it was the emperor, and no longer the pope, who was vicar of Jesus Christ. The Church was thus but an annex to the State; the feudal system had enriched her, but it had also enslaved her. It had stripped her of her ecumenical character to make her an institution of caste. The pope was nothing but an imperial chaplain. The bishops were but court chaplains:—the hierarchy was open only to the scions of great families. There arose an ecclesiastical feudalism as there was a military feudalism—both recruited from the same class. The Church leaned upon the powerful ones of the world; she shared their wealth and their authority; it would seem that her destinies were linked indissolubly to those of feudalism. One might say that like the people of Israel, like the Roman Empire, feudalism had wished to dominate the Church, and that, more fortunate than these, it had succeeded.

Evil results of Lay Investiture.

This situation was grave beyond precedent, both for the welfare of the Church herself and for her influence upon the nations. From the moment the choice of prelates, instead of being regulated by rigorous canonical prescriptions, depended solely on the arbitrary power of the kings, it was no longer priestly virtue which opened the ranks of the episcopate. The great question was to give to the sovereign guarantees of fidelity to his dynasty and to his politics, or to be endorsed by his courtiers. But the courtiers no longer gave their protection gratuitously; they sold it. Most of the bishops, therefore, bought their office, and, naturally, once they had acquired it, they endeavored to indemnify themselves by selling in their turn the dignities of secondary order. The inferior clergy, on their side, in order to re-imburse themselves, sold the sacraments, and in this manner, from the top to the bottom of the ladder, the grace of the redemption was sold at auction. The temple of God out of which Jesus had driven the sellers had become a den of thieves.

But, of all abuses, this kind of traffic was the one the Church condemned the most severely, and the one against which she had formulated most of her anathemas. From the dawn of Christianity, she had indignantly stigmatized it—from the day when Simon the magician offered money to St. Peter to obtain the power of imposition of hands, and drew from the Prince of the Apostles this thundering reply: "Keep thy money to thyself to perish with thee!" (*) From that day on the name of simony has been given to traffic in sacred things, and all generations have renewed the prohibition of this sacrilegious practice.

And, of course, a simoniacal clergy did not worry much about the virtues of its vocation. Having entered Holy Orders, for the most part, in order to obtain a suitable position, they enjoyed the good things of life, indulged in high living, took part in all worldly distractions, festivities, games, hunting, and even war. A very large number of priests showed their love for the sacraments by receiving two that are incompatible: Holy Orders and Matrimony! They lived openly as fathers of families, surrounded by their wives and children, and they considered celibacy an antiquated custom no longer to be observed. Needless to say these pretended marriages, forbidden by canon law, were in the eyes of the Church nothing but shameful concubinages.

You may imagine the influence which a clergy so degraded could exert upon the people whom it was their duty to instruct and uplift. The most powerful of all teaching is

---

* The Acts VIII-20.

example:—but their example taught the people to trample under foot, with cynicism or without conscience, the most formal precepts of the religion of which they were the ministers. We who, by the grace of God, live in a time when the clergy, by the admirable dignity of their lives, bear testimony to the truth of their teachings, can hardly imagine the sad condition of the faithful of those days, who saw the priesthood invaded by men who lived in concubinage and who were traffickers in the sacraments. When luxury and venality had their seats in the sanctuary and talked from the pulpits, what could be the feelings of the hearers? Christ said to His first priests: "You are the salt of the earth. But if the salt lose its savor, wherewith shall it be salted?" These words found a sad application in the society of those days. Social progress had come to a standstill, and the Christian world went backwards. Some of the faithful—and these the more barbarous— quietly followed in the footsteps of their pastors and plunged into the mire of all vices; others—and these the more logical—turned away with disgust from a religion which they saw represented by such ministers. Both classes were, so to say, ripe for a religious revolution which would have snatched them away from the influence of Christianity. Heresy could confidently knock at their door: —it was sure to find admission.

Albigensian heresy.

And indeed, from the beginning of the eleventh century we see heresy everywhere—and such heresy! A doctrine disastrous, lugubrious, horrible as sin and as death! A dark night which came down with the weight of lead and with the coldness of ice upon the mind and upon the heart, a chancre of death which ate at all the luminous and elevated faculties of the human soul, a deadly folly that choked the joy of living and made existence here below like a bad dream:—such was the heresy of the Albigenses! Compare it not to any other heresy:—all others left standing the sacred banner of hope, kept the faith in Christ the Redeemer, maintained in the souls of men the high and manly conviction that life is worth living, that the struggle between good and evil will finally close in keeping with the demands of human conscience. According to the Albigensian heresy, on the contrary, there was certainty of salvation, neither through the Church which they held worthy of all contempt, nor through the Redeemer who according to them had been subject to the law of sin, nor through the law of God who in their opinion was not almighty, but opposed by an evil principle whose power equaled His own. Instead of the harmony, the equilibrium, the order, which the Christian faith sees in the rule of the Divine Wisdom throughout the universe, the Albigensian perceived nothing but an atrocious struggle between good and evil, fighting for possession of the world in a duel, whose tragical stake was the soul of man.

The Albigensian held that the Christian faith was vain and the Redemption but a lure; that evil was an eternal principle and that the created world, with all its splendors, was its work. He maintained that it was man's own fault if he was composed of a soul and a body—the soul the work of the good god, and the body the work of the evil god. The soul, he said, had been lured into the body by the seductions of the evil god; it was imprisoned there, and its only hope of salvation was to leave it at any cost. Hence suicide was a religious act, since it liberated the soul; hence marriage was to be disapproved because, by reproduction, it perpetuated indefinitely the captivity of souls in the bodies. One sees here collective suicide, the monstrous tenet of a modern philosophy, vaguely advocated as the only solution.

Such were the leading features of the pernicious doctrine which dried up the supernatural life of humanity at its source and plunged the human conscience into the dread darkness whence Christ had called it unto the light of the Redemption. Alas! the men of that epoch must have felt sorely forsaken, sorely disabused of the Christian ideal or they would not, in their despair, have cast themselves in so large numbers into the arms of

such a religion! And yet day by day it spread
wider and wider. Like one of those deadly
scourges which in the past came from Asia,
it advanced little by little: the historian can
follow on the map the progress of its itiner-
ary of death covering every land as with a
pall.

It is called the Albigensian heresy, and we
know for a fact that at a certain moment its
principle forces were concentrated about Albi
in the South of France. But have no illusion
on the subject, it was everywhere. It was
in the north, at Arras, at Liége and in the center of France, at Châlons, at Orléans, that it
exhibited its most ancient manifestations.
Hidden often under the most inoffensive ex-
terior, it was difficult to recognize it at first
sight in any particular sect; of harmless appearance, as in the case of the earlier Waldenses (*) it gradually and fatally invaded all
centers where the disappearance of Catholic
faith had left a void, and legions of men lived
under its shadow, never realizing that the mutilated Christianity of which they made profession was but a branch of the Mani-
chean trunk. All the sects of that time

(*) The Waldenses   derived their   name from Peter
Waldo, a rich merchant of Lyons, who gathered around him
a number of followers and sent them out two by two to
preach in the country districts about Lyons (A. D. 1170).
Alexander III praised their zeal, but recommended that they
should not interfere with the duties of the clergy. They paid
no attention to this advice and were excommunicated at the
Council Verona (A. D. 1184). Their rebellion against the
Church naturally led the Waldenses into heresy.

were like so many lateral canals which discharged their waters into the central sewer of Manicheism (*). Directly or indirectly, all the other heresies were its tributaries. They swarmed everywhere. A thousand extravagant and scandalous sects sprang into existence, hideous vermin which covered the poor sick body of society. Among a populace on the verge of frenzy, but still feeling the need of religion, the fiercest of heresiarchs, the vilest of charlatans found a welcome and a hearing. As proof if this I mention the wretch, Tanchelm, who had chosen the city of Antwerp as his field of operation. Such was the fanatical enthusiasm of his followers that—excuse the repugnant detail—they went the length of drinking the water in which he had washed himself. One day he announced that he was going to marry the Blessed Virgin and that he had placed an offering box on either side of the door at the house where the ceremony was to take place; he wished to know—from the liberality they would show in filling them —which of his followers, men or women, were the more devoted to him. Both boxes were filled.

If, as I have said a while ago, it is not always easy to detect the hidden relationship

---

(*) Manicheism was propogated by Manes, who was born in Persia in 240. He announced himself as a new apostle of Jesus Christ and proclaimed the existence of two eternal principles—a good and an evil principle.

which connected all the sects of the time with
the leading heresy, there was nevertheless a
very apparent family trait among them all;—
and that was their boundless aversion for the
clergy. And this brings us back, by a round-
about way that has not failed to be instruct-
ive, to the origin which I have assigned to
this dreadful inundation of heresy:—the cor·
ruption of the clergy. It was the scandal of
simoniacal and concubinary priests that
opened the door through which the multitudes
rushed headlong out of the Church.

Restoration of Christian spirit among clergy.

It might have seemed, accordingly, that
Christianity and civilization were running
into bankruptcy. But the Catholic Church
is made for eternal renewals. Sometimes it
might appear that the sources of grace and
of life coming down upon her from the heav-
enly heights lose themselves and run waste
in the distance; but, no!—at a given moment
they gush forth from her bosom in columns
so much the higher for having been buried
the deeper, to spread about her in refreshing
and life-giving streams. And this was what
men actually saw in those dark days. The
inexhaustible vitality of the Church, under
the impure flood of heresy, withdrew and concentrated towards her heart; there she drew
a greater intensity and energy, and prepared
to enter by vigorous pulsations into all the

arteries and veins of this great suffering body.

Meanwhile she lived a refugee in the cloisters, those perpetual asylums of the persecuted Christian spirit. All the cloisters had not remained equally free from corruption, but, from the beginning of the tenth century, an active reform movement had originated in those of Lorraine and of Burgundy. Reformers had appeared who had dreamed of restoring to monastic life all its ideal perfection and who succeeded in their efforts. Thus at Gorcy, at Brogne, at Cluny especially, there were centers of monastic reform and regeneration whose activities radiated into the distance. Cluny, which had the good fortune to have at its head for more than a century a succession of eminent men, has left its name to this movement. The disciples and the admirers of the Cluniac school carried its ideas and its reform into all the lands of Western Europe. To be just, one must note also the part in the work of reform due to the illustrious Italian ascetics, such as St. Romuald, the founder of the Camaldolese, St. John Gualbert, the founder of Vallombrosa, St. Nilus, who won over to the attraction of the religious life the Emperor Otho III himself, and who, perhaps, might have induced him to lay down the crown if death had not freed the young prince from this heavy burden.

All these monastic hearths, shining forth

one after another like the stars of heaven,
preserved and fed the sacred fire of the
Christian spirit; they restored an atmosphere
where all those who had held to the ideal of
the gospel and who had not despaired of the
future gathered to refresh themselves. The
ranks of the Militant Church were formed
anew about the monasteries; the secular clergy,
in turn, furnished doctors and advocates
to the cause of the reform. Such was the
magnanimous Wazon, Bishop of Liége, the
first to define with absolute precision the
principles which have been called Gregorian,
but which it would suffice to call Catholic.
Such again was the noble Anselm of Lucca,
the great and exemplary bishop, who became
pope under the name Alexander II, and who
was destined to be one of the most deserving
of the precursors of Gregory VII (*), And
there were many others. They all had their

(*)   Gregory VII (Hildebrand) was born in Italy, about
1020; died May 25, 1085. During the reign of Pope Leo IX
he showed great executive ability and a burning desire for
reform. At the death of Leo IX, asked by the people and
clergy of Rome to become Pope, he had Victor II elected
instead. During the reign of this Pontiff he steadily maintained and even increased the ascendency which his com-
manding genius had acquired for him during the pontificate of Leo IX. At the death of Victor II Hildebrand secured the election of Nicholas II. The decree of election of
Pope Nicholas by which the power of choosing the Pope is
vested in the College of Cardinals was in a large measure
the achievement of Hildebrand, whose power and influence
had become supreme in Rome. At the obsequies of Alexander
II, whom Hildebrand's influence had raised to the pontificate,
a loud outcry from the whole multitude of clergy and people
was heard: "Let Hildebrand be Pope!" On the same day
Hildebrand was conducted to the Church of San Pietro in
Vincoli, and there elected in canonical form by the assembled
Cardinals.

eyes fixed on the Roman See; over the heads
of the corrupt episcopacy, all asked of the
pope the salvation of the world. To use the
modern expression, they were ultramontane
in the fullest sense of the word.

Reforms demanded.

These men, scattered everywhere, lent the
prestige of a life above reproach to elevated
and pure doctrines; and little by little, they
compelled public interest; it may be said that
they formed public opinion in the centers
where religious and social problems were discussed. Their activities were not confined to
the ranks of the clergy; they recruited adherents from all classes of society, even from
among the princes and the crowned heads.
One of them was the powerful Emperor of
Germany, Henry III, the pitiless opponent
of simony and Nicolaitanism. No one has
branded those abuses with more bitterness,
no one has fought them with more vigor. He
took care to intrust episcopal sees only to
men above reproach, and those whom his influence raised to the chair of Peter—Clement
II and Damasus II—were worthy of it beyond contradiction. This may seem strange
on the part of a sovereign who more than any
other held to his pretended right of lay investiture; but it is easy to explain. In human
society, it is one thing to notice an abuse, and
another thing to detect its source. The obser-

vations which we make at a distance—in the
light of history and with all the documentary
evidence under our eyes—could not have been
made with the same facility by the people who
lived in those days, who were in the midst of
the fray, who saw only a portion of the facts
and who, moreover, were inclined, by self-
interest and by their condition in life, to
see these facts in a different light.   This
is why there were in those days—as there
are now—good people who, though lamenting
the abuses of society, would have indignantly
rejected the remedy, had it been proposed to
them.

Difficulty of situation.

What was this remedy? As I have said before, it did not consist in the prohibition pure
and simple of simony and concubinage.   As
long as they handed over episcopal sees to
men given to simony and concubinage, their
vices would occupy the sees with them.   The
true remedy was to prevent such men from
penetrating by stratagem into the fold, from
entering, as the saying is, otherwise than by
the door. To this end it was necessary again
to put in force the canonical prescriptions
concerning the election of Church dignitaries;
in other words, it was necessary to restore to
the Church her liberty and to respect the
distinction of the two powers by taking from
the kings the power of investiture. This was

very simple—it is the very simplicity of the
idea that made it dreadful and made it appear chimerical. To deny to princes a privilege to which clung the best as well as the
worst, would have let loose the most terrible
of wars, a war which Christian society had
not known to that day—the war between
Church and State. And this war would have
been not only a war against the kings but
also a struggle against the feudal class,
against all that rich and powerful society
which supported and favored the Church in
its own way, and without which it seemed
that she would be doomed to absolute power-
lessness. It would have provoked among the
hierarchy itself a furious and desperate resistance on the part of all the prelates who
owed their dignity to lay investiture and
whose titles to possession would have become
imperiled by the anathema cast upon their
origin. These were frightful anticipations
which of necessity disturbed the minds of the
reformers. And it is not astonishing that
more than one recoiled before such eventu-
alities.

Tact of Leo IX. and successors.

Nevertheless the Catholic Church did not
hesitate. But with what tact, with what
prudence, with what caution did she proceed
at first! To proclaim the true principles and
to insist upon their application would have

been useless, since they were not known; and
it would have been dangerous, since they were
not recognized.   She did better:—little by
little she re-accustomed the minds of the people
to respect those principles, by affirming tac-
itly the right through precedents which she
created when she had the power to do so,
making those principles prevail, without show,
indeed, but with all the more vigor.   An example will show how this reform proceeded.

In 1048, the pontifical throne became vacant and the emperor Henry III designated
as its incumbent his cousin Bruno, who was
then bishop of Toul and who is known in
history as Leo IX.   He belonged to that
group of zealous and fervent Christians who
dreamed of the regeneration of the Church.
He did not protest against his selection; he
did not say to his cousin's face that he
had not the right to dispose of the chair of
Peter, and that he, as a bishop, could not consider himself pope except he were elected by
the clergy of Rome in accordance with the
rules of Canon Law.   Such language would
have spoiled it all:—Henry III, angered,
would have named another pope, who, probably, would have been more compliant and
the great work of the reform would not
have taken place.   But what Leo IX did
not express in words, he proclaimed by his
conduct with not less power, and with more
gentleness than if he had spoken.   He at

once set out to take possession of the pontifical see, but he left as a simple pilgrim, without retinue, staff in hand, praying and fasting on the way; he walked into Rome barefooted and it was only after he had been elected in accordance with the rules of Canon Law that he donned the pontifical insignia and acted as the head of the Church. Thus lay investiture was quietly weakened by the very person who received it, and this without the least conflict. The two successors of Leo IX conformed to his example, and, after a few years, the idea of the liberty of the Apostolic See became so much a matter of course that, in 1059, Pope Nicholas II could take a further step and publish his celebrated constitution on the election of sovereign pontiffs.

Nicholas II regulates election of sovereign pontiffs.

This constitution was a model of energy and cleverness. On the one hand it loudly proclaimed the law and decreed that the pope should be elected by the college of cardinals; on the other hand, it wisely took cognizance of the facts and decided that the ruling emperor, and each of his successors to whom the Church would grant the privilege, should have the right to confirm the election. This concession—intended solely to take care of the transition period—soon fell into disuse, and the constitution of 1059 alone remained in force. It may be fitting to remark here that its dispositions are still in force; it was in accordance with them that the present Pope—Benedict XV—was elected and that his successor will be elected. All will admit that an electoral law which lasts for eight and a half centuries is a rather rare phenomenon of longevity, and one which it would be difficult to find outside of the Catholic Church.

Gregory VII. proscribes lay investiture.

Thus was the Papacy emancipated; it then put itself to the task of liberating the Church. This is its traditional mission, in accordance with the word spoken to Peter: "but thou being converted confirm thy brethren." All eyes were turned towards the Sovereign Pontiff; having seen him set free, the Christian world then asked him to act. From the bosom of the Church there arose weighty voices begging him to save society. St. Peter Damian, in a way, echoed them all. Dreadful hour! Painful hesitation! Would the Papacy rise to the occasion? Would it dare look the all powerful evil in the face, and, having viewed it from all angles, strike it down? Would it dare pronounce the supreme word which, once spoken, could not be revoked, the word which would be the signal for the universal conflagration? This question was asked at the moment when there had just ascended the Chair of Peter one who had been the soul of all reforms for a generation. He was known

then as the Monk Hildebrand; to-day he is
known as Pope Gregory VII. He stood there,
on the border line between the past and the
future, a man who separates the cent'i-
ries. He stood ready, lance in hand, knowing
that his action would be answered by a thousand confused and terrible cries—the noise
either of a falling or of a resurgent world.

I imagine that when Pope Gregory was
about to deliver the supreme stroke, he felt
his hand tremble. This intrepid reformer—
perhaps the most intrepid of men—must then
have felt that sacred terror and weakening
of the flesh which was not spared Jesus Himself in the Garden of Olives. There is nothing
more august and more touching than the
voluntary sacrifice made by those whom God
has chosen to execute a great mission; they
are conscious that they are to be its first victims, but nevertheless they act. Thus, when
in 1075 Gregory VII formulated against lay
investiture the prohibition which he accentuated in 1078 and in 1080, and when he for-
bade even kings and emperors to confer any
religious dignity, he attained the acme of
moral grandeur in his whole career. Never,
neither in the passing eclat of his triumph,
nor in the magnanimous patience displayed
amid the tribulations of his exile, did Gregory VII do any thing more sublime than
when he made this proclamation, which was

about to plunge him into the abyss of endless trouble.

The war which was then kindled lasted fifty years, and neither Gregory VII nor Henry IV lived to see its end. I need not tell you its story—you will find its details in the textbooks of history; my task is to make you realize its bearing. It was a furious struggle, in which were engaged all Christian peoples, all classes of society. It deeply disturbed a world still young and passionate. It set loose an avalanche of pamphlets in which everything was attacked with a violence heretofore unknown in doctrinal debate. In the course of the conflict there were strange surrenders and strange and sudden changes, and shameful waverings in the most manly characters. The good cause, attacked with unprecedented fury, was often compromised by the extreme measures of its own defenders, and the revolutionary spirit was aided, more than once, by appearing to operate under the auspices of authority. And, in such encounters, the distracted conservatives could turn in anger to the Sovereign Pontiff, and say to him: "Behold your partisans, and behold your work!"

And, as often happens, they unscrupulously identified the reformers with the revolutionaries. As an instance of this we may cite that generous Catholic democracy of Milan, which was guided by St. Arialdo and St.

Erlembaldo, but which was branded by its opponents with the name of Cathari—a name,
however, which it transformed into a title of
honor. The storm which disturbed everything
seemed to bring darkness into the minds of men
and decadence into Christian society. The
Papacy however remained undisturbed in the
midst of the universal upheaval. Gregory
VII died at Salerno, Victor III fled from
Rome on the day of his consecration, Urban
II prepared the first crusade in the midst of
his struggles, Pascal II languished in the
prisons of Henry V; but the Papacy, looking
beneath the convulsions of the surface, saw
arising the harvests of the future. Under the
wind of the storm the truths which it had
sown grew up in the conscience of the nations.
The vital principles of Christianity little by
little unfolded their conclusions in formulas
of luminous and energetic precision, and
slowly succeeded in taking possession of men's
minds. Leaning upon the elite of the regular
and secular clergy, upheld by the ever growing adherence of the multitudes, served by
pure devotedness—such as that of the Countess Mathilda of Tuscany, (*) known as the

---

(*) Countess Mathilda of Tuscany, or of Canossa,
1046-1114, was finely educated, deeply religious and from her
youth followed with interest the great ecclesiastical questions
of the day. Her domains were of the greatest importance
in the political and ecclesiastical disputes of the time, as
the road from Germany to Rome, by way of upper Italy,
passed through them. On the 22d of April, 1073, Gregory VII.
became pope and before long the great battle for the independence of the Church and the reform of ecclesiastical life
began. In this contest Mathilda was the fearless, courageous,
generous and unswerving ally of Gregory and his successors.
It was at Mathilda's mountain stronghold of Canossa that
Henry IV. appeared before Gregory VII. and atoned for his
guilt by public penance.

Joan of Arc of the Papacy—the Holy See
held firm.

Gregory VII. triumphs.

In fact, thirty-seven years after his death,
Gregory VII triumphed from the depth of his
grave. In the Concordat of Worms, in 1122, the
Church compelled the State to recognize the
right for which she had fought so hard. The
State gave back to her the freedom of her
canonical elections, from that of the pope
down to the elections of all the inferior dignitaries; the Church remained sovereign in
her own domain.   In mixed questions she
made concessions in accordance with her custom.

Free thenceforth to devote herself entirely
to the great work of reform, she displayed an
energy and an activity without limit.   In less
than a century, she extinguished Manicheism;
she sent all Europe to the Crusades; she drew
forth from her bosom three new orders, the
first for the ministry of souls (1), the second for the preaching of doctrine (2), the

---

(1)   The Cistercian order is named after its first mon-
astery at Citeaux (Cistercium) in France, where the society
was founded in 1098 by St. Robert, under the rule of St.
Benedict.   St. Bernard was the most celebrated member of
the order, and is considered as its second founder.   In 1134,
after thirty-six years of existence, the order counted seventy
monasteries.   The Cistersians led a contemplative and very
ascetic life.

(2)   St. Dominic, born in Spain in 1170, founded the
Order of the Friars Preachers or Dominicans, in 1215.   At
the first general chapter held at Bologna in 1220 it was determined that the habit of the Friars Preachers, theretofore
called Black Friars, should be white and that the order
should possess no property.

third for the practice of poverty (1). She presided at the birth of communes and universities, she covered with her prestige Gothic art (2) and scholasticism (3), she saw saints ascend the thrones of France (4) and of Cas-

---

(1) For the practice of poverty St. Francis of Assisi, born in Italy in 1182, founded the Friars Minor or Minorites. Its principal object is the realization of a poverty so perfect that it should be manifested in every way and in all things. The order was formally approved by Honorius III in 1223.

(2) Gothic Art. The word Gothic designates the style of architecture which flournished in the western part of Europe from the end of the twelfth century to the revival of the classical styles in the sixteenth century. Generally speaking, the Gothic style is at once the most scientific and the most artistic style of architecture. It is the most scientific, because its whole strength is made to reside in a finely organized and frankly confessed framework rather than in walls. This framework, made up of piers, arches and buttresses, is freed from every unnecessary incumbrance of wall and it is rendered as light in all its parts as is compatible with strength. It is the most artistic style because the liberal, harmonious and consistent use of the pointed arch, the trefoil, the quatrefoil, the cinquefoil, foliated capitals, deep mouldings, finials, crockets, four-petaled flowers, etc., enable the artist to make our Gothic buildings, pictures of perfect beauty. The Gothic monuments of the Middle Ages are at once the admiration and the despair of modern architects.

(3) Scholasticism. This term denotes the method or system of teaching and the doctrines of "The Schoolmen" or philosophers and theologians of the Middle Ages, especially from the eleventh to the sixteenth centuries. They reduced into unity and system the teachings of the philosophers and theologians who had gone before them. The greatest among them was St. Thomas. He is called the "Angel of the School." Pope Leo XIII. of glorious memory, in his encyclical "Aeterni Patris Filius" urged the Christian world to return to the study of philosophy and theology in accordance with St. Thomas.

(4) The author here alludes to St. Louis, king of France, who undertook two crusades against the Mohammedans and died of fever in 1270, in the course of his second crusade, in his camp near Carthage.

tile (*). And, during two centuries, the
twelfth and thirteenth, she became the supreme authority of Western Europe, the oracle of the Christian world.

A turning point in history of Church.

Such were the results of the generous reaction whereby the Catholic Church saved her
future.   To do this she had to tear herself
away from the embrace of feudalism, which
desired to make of her a religion of camp
chapels and connect her with its fleeting
destinies. In comparing the Christian Church
as it was at the eve of the conflict with what
it has been since, one can realize the bearing
of this great phenomenon and understand
that there is no exaggeration in seeing in this
salutary crisis one of the turning points of
the history of civilization.

(*)   St. Ferdinand III (1219-1252) conquered the greater
part of Andalusia, leaving the Mohammedans only the king-
dome of Granada.   The cathedral of Burgos occupies the first
place among the monuments of his greatness.

The Church and Neo=Caesarism (*)

The Church emerged victorious from the conflict of the Investitures. Being now free from the abuses which had dishonored her she attained unwonted prestige. The Papacy was like the sun at its zenith: supreme arbiter of the moral and religious life of the peoples; there was no social interest which was foreign to Rome.

The Church at its zenith.

How did the Church use her influence? She had a twofold aim: to pacify Europe and to turn her united forces against Islam. The Popes pursued this sublime ideal with magnificent courage and abnegation. Peace among the Christian peoples was their constant care, just as peace among the individuals had been the special concern of the bishops who, in the tenth and the eleventh centuries, succeeded in establishing the Truce

---

(*)   Neo-Caesarism means new Caesarism. Caesarism is derived from the word Caesar, the Roman general and dictator (B. C. 100-44) and designates a system of government in which unrestricted power is exercised by a single person. "Kaiserism" is the modern and shorter term for Neo-Caesarism.

of God (1). It was also a truce of God of which the Papacy dreamed—no longer a truce between individuals, but a truce between nations. The Papacy desired this truce, in the first place, for the thing itself, since human civilization has no higher aim than peace. She desired it, in the second place, that she might oppose a compact and united Europe against the eternal enemy—the Crescent (2). And note well, this dream of the Popes of the Middle Ages has remained the inheritance of generous minds, from Joan of Arc and Christopher Columbus down to Leibnitz and Cardinal Lavigerie. And we may hope that it will also be the ideal of Europe, when a re-christianized Europe will have become reconciled with the ideal.

The splendor of the social role of the Papacy at this epoch found majestic expression

---

(1) The Truce of God was a temporary suspension of hostilities. It was brought into existence to curb the war lust of the feudal lords. A Council of Elne in 1207, in a canon concerning the sanctification of Sunday, forebade hostilities from Saturday night until Monday morning. This prohibition was subsequently extended to the days of the week consecrated by the great mysteries of Christianity, namely, Thursday in memory of the Ascension, Friday, the day of the Passion—Still another step included Advent and Lent in the Truce. The penalty for the violation of the Truce was excommunication. The Truce soon spread from France to Germany and Italy. The ecumenical council of 1179 extended the institution to the whole Church.

(2) The Crescent, or sign of the increasing moon, was the ancient symbol of Byzantium or Constantinople. After the taking of that city by the Turks in 1453, it became the emblem of the Turkish Empire and the sign and symbol of the Mohammedan religion, just as the Cross is the emblem of the Christian religion.

during the festivities of the First Jubilee, which was celebrated in Rome, in 1300, whilst Boniface VIII occupied the chair of Peter. During the course of that year, the Pope, from the windows of his palace, saw the Christian world pass before him, going to the tombs of the Apostles in order to gain the indulgences of the Jubilee. The Eternal City then presented an incredible spectacle:—there were never fewer than two hundred thousand visitors, a truly astounding number if we consider the primitive modes of travel of those days. An eyewitness has described for us, in immortal verse, these vast throngs crossing the bridge of St. Angelo on their way to and from the Vatican; those going held the right, those coming back the left, as is done at the present day on the bridges of the large German cities. And painting, as well as poetry, has immortalized this spectacle, for one of the most ancient paintings of Giotto—which may be seen to the present day in the Church of St. John Lateran—is his Boniface VIII proclaiming the Jubilee from the loggia of that sanctuary. Certainly in this year of boundless enthusiasm, when the Pope almost seemed to be more than a mere man and saw the whole of mankind at his feet, he needed an act of profound humility to resist the suggestions of such high fortune; more than once he had need to recall the words pro-

nounced on the day of his coronation whilst
they burned the tow at the foot of the Pontifical throne: "Holy Father, thus passeth the
glory of this world."

**Rule of Christian society wrested from Pope by Lay
State.**

And indeed, thus passed the glory of this
world for Boniface VIII. Before his death,
this old man, at the age of seventy-seven, had
to assist at the catastrophe which threatened
to engulf the incomparable destinies of the
Papacy. Two years after the triumph of the
great Jubilee, the mercenaries of the Most
Christian King seized the Vicar of Christ in
his own palace, and the nation which called
herself the eldest daughter of the Church
attempted to crush the Roman See. The
Pope, when on the brink of the grave, over-
whelmed with sorrow and humiliation, knew
that a dreadful revolution was consummated,
or at least that its principle had been triumphantly affirmed, and that, for centuries
to come, the rule of human society had been
wrested from the Vicar of Jesus Christ (*).

Who then was the mysterious and terrible
enemy that was about to upset Christian
Europe, paralyze the action of the Papacy
and change the course of civilization? It

(*) The author refers here to Philip hte Fair, king of
France, sending William of Nogaret to Anagni in order to
seize Pope Boniface VIII.

was the Lay State, a new and conquering
power which preceding centuries had not
known. It rose suddenly, like a giant, to
face the Papacy and provoke it to mortal
combat. Armed from the beginning with a
theory from which it deduced its omnipotence,
this Lay State claimed the adherence of its
followers with the authority of an unquestion-
able dogma, though in reality it had no other
principle than force; it began against the
Church of Christ the long drawn out combat
which has not yet neared its end, and whose
fluctuating fortunes remained for our de-
scendants the most solemn problem of history.

Limited authority of kings becomes absolute.

This gives me occasion once more to recall
that it is ideas which rule the world. It is in
the incorporeal region of the mind that are
worked out those irresistible forces which
destroy or build up:—just as yonder, on the
silent and solitary summits of the Alps, are
formed the streams which flow down to the
valleys, to bring them life, when their course
is tranquil, but to work devastation, when
swollen by the storms.

Let us, in turn, go up to the summits, to dis-
cover how, in the region of ideas, there was
worked out the political doctrine which was
about to fall like an avalanche on this growing society. At first sight, this theory seems
opposed to the spirit of the Middle Ages.

To the men of this epoch, the king was without doubt the head of society, and religion invested him with a sacred and inviolable character. But his authority was far from being unlimited; everywhere—in the stronghold of the nobleman, in the walled enclosure of the communes, under the vaults of the churches and monasteries, on the lofty throne of St. Peter—it met free forces which acted as a counterpoise and did not permit the king to exceed the limits established by religion and by custom. The king of the Middle Ages was what would to-day be termed a constitutional king, not that there always existed written documents which formally limited his power, but because the privileges of the various classes of society were, in effect, a limit which he might not overstep, if he did not wish to hear the voice of public anger grumbling about his throne.

If this was the case, how could the idea of royal absolutism, at a given moment, take hold of the minds of men and finally triumph to such a point that it eliminated from modern politics the influence of the Church and of its Head? The question is very complex; I will endeavor, nevertheless, to answer it with clearness and precision.

Royal absolutism due to ultra-nationalism and adoption of Roman law.

Manifestly, there is among modern peoples —to some extent among all peoples—an in-

vincible repugnance to international governments. Each nation seeks within itself the
sovereign principle of its activity; it obeys
with pleasure only the authorities which have
emanated from its bosom; it is tempted to
regard as a stranger a master living at too
great a distance. If by their sacred character,
by the necessary universality which is part of
dogma itself, the religious institutions escape
this centrifugal tendency, this is not true of
political institutions which nations will not
support except on condition that they have
them under full control. This explains the
dismemberment of the empire of Charlemagne, which was regretted by only a few
cultured minds. We may thus understand
why for centuries Italy opposed the authority
of its emperors. These national tendencies,
however little they were excited, became
passions, and when aroused by an interested
power, these passions knew no bounds. "The
Pope or the King, which is to be the ruler of
the kingdom of France?" The query, thus
put, could receive but one answer, and the
best Christians, questioned in this way, sided
spontaneously with the king and espoused his
cause against the Chief of Christendom, for
the defense of the national liberties. To this
influence of national self-love, whose power it
would be difficult to exaggerate, there was
added another force which was not less powerful. At this time all intellectual and scien-

tific superiority was not confined to the
ranks of the clergy. A lay society had come
into existence and had developed; it had its
superior minds, its scientists, its jurists, its
statesmen; it was conscious of its power and
of its dignity; it took its place alongside of
the ecclesiastical order, it had no intention of
leaving to the latter the exclusive direction of
minds, and already it had taken a prominent
part in politics and legislation.

Thus nationalism, on the one part, laicism,
on the other part, without being hostile in
principle to the Church, had nevertheless a
different ideal and pursued a course which
was easily set against the aims of the
Church. But this opposition, in order to become conscious and intense, needed to be
stirred up by some resolute agent; this agent
was at hand. We shall see him at work.

The Middle Ages had at all times a strong
predilection for the study of antiquity. They
put all the more ardor into the study because
antiquity was, at this epoch, almost the only
object of scientific knowledge. This study
gave them an opportunity of knowing another
society, a civilization different from theirs.
This society appeared to them through the
radiant prism of its masterpieces, with the
magical colors of a better world. Thus the
poets and philosophers of antiquity enjoyed,
during the Middle Ages, an authority second

only to that of the Gospel. Aristotle (1) was the fetich of the school, the master of those who know, and when his authority had been invoked—Magister dixit—the last word had been spoken. As to Virgil—it did not suffice to honor him as the prince of poets; he had become a marvelous personage, half magician, half prophet. Sometimes, this infatuation literally turned the heads of people, as happened in the case of that poor monk of the tenth century who, six hundred years before Don Quixote, took for realities the fictions of Virgil (2) and taught that the only true religion was that of the Aeneid!

Nowhere did this fetichism for antiquity manifest itself in more extravagant ways and nowhere did it produce more disastrous results than among the men given to the study of law, the jurists, as they were called. I shall confine myself to just one example of this intellectual malady. In accordance with the chroniclers, a manuscript of the Pandects

---

(1) Aristotle (384-322 B. C.) Greek philosopher, a pupil of Plato, teacher of Alexander the Great, is considered the greatest heathen philosopher. He wrote the first systematic treatise on logic. He wrote also treatises on metaphysics, physics, biology, zoology, psychology, anthropology, ethics, politics, poetry and rhetoric.

(2) Virgil, (70-19 B. C.) a famous Roman poet. His "Aeneid" is the greatest of Latin epics.

(*) preserved at Florence was venerated as a relic. People came on pilgrimage to see it. and two men, each holding a lighted candle in hand, stood, one to the right, the other to the left of the show-window where the much revered conjuring book received the homage of its devotees. This is sheer burlesque. A more serious phase of it is that from the eleventh century, the first law school in Europe, that of Bologna, propagated in the Occident the cult of *Corpus Juris Civilis* and refused thenceforth to recognize any other source of jurisprudence. The national law of the modern peoples was despised and derided by the jurists who prided themselves on their acquaintance with the masterpiece of Justinian, and thus it fell more and more into disuse. Meanwhile the Roman law began its triumphant course which was to end in the conquest of all Christendom. This infatuation for the Roman law may be explained partly by the incontestable superiority, which, under some aspects, it had over the Germanic law of the Middle Ages. The latter, born of ancient Barbarian customs, preserved the stamp of the rudimentary society of which it was the expression. Written in

---

(*) By "Pandects" is meant the digest, or abridgment, in fifty books, of the decisions, writings and opinions of the old Roman jurists, made in the sixth century by direction of the Emperor Justinian, and forming the leading compilation of the Roman civil law. It is also called "Corpus Juris" (body of the law.)

crude language, it was almost exclusively
penal and left unsolved most of the complex
problems which result from the social relations of civilized men. It was devoid of all
prestige in the eyes of the learned, it lacked
the authority which comes from association
with the name of a great jurist, it resembled
one of these close fitting and curtailed gar-
ments which may suit a child but impede the
gait of the adult. The Roman law, on the
contrary, evolved during centuries by generations of learned men, appeared as a great
monument, firm of foundation and indestructible in workmanship. It had the amplitude,
the richness, the scientific precision worthy
of a great civilization. In it all was foreseen,
analyzed and judged by a luminous and profound intelligence which seemed to have pene-
trated the entire social life and which had
acquired some sort of universality and infallibility. The Roman people, pre-eminently a
juridical people, have produced nothing
greater than the Roman law; and if one wishes
to form an idea of the Roman people in the
work which best represents their genius, one
must study them in their legislative work. It
is not astonishing, therefore, that the minds of
men in the Middle Ages should have been
dazzled at this aspect of the Roman law—much
the same as the travelers of that period,
who came from the northern cities before
the erection of our great cathedrals, were

wont to stop overawed at the sight of the
Column of Trajan, the Coliseum, or the Baths
of Caracalla. And as there is but a step from
admiration to imitation, it is no wonder that
the Middle Ages took the step and dreamed
of making the *Corpus Juris Civilis* the code
of the civilized world at that time.

Roman law fosters unbridled absolutism or Caesarism.

Here began the deplorable and tragical error. While from a scientific point of view,
the Roman law was incontestably superior to
the laws of the Middle Ages; while, with regard to civil relations, it displayed a perfection which the barbarian codes could not
approach; on the other hand, from a pontical
point of view, it enshrined a system from
which, it seems, the minds of the free men of
the Middle Ages should have turned away
with horror. The most unbridled absolutism
was proclaimed as a doctrine with unprecedented boldness and logic. According to the
Roman law, the sovereign, that is, the emperor,
was a veritable god. Not that the Roman
sceptics and the unbelievers of the Empire
imagined that he really possessed a divine
nature—they knew the contrary but too well
—but they conceded that he possessed over
his subjects the same power that God Himself
has over His creatures. The will of the emperor took the place of justice and law, or, to
express it better, his will was law. And though

that will was ordinarily but a cruel and depraved caprice, as in the case of such tyrants as Caligula (1), Nero (2), Domitian (3), Commodus (4), Caracalla (5), Heliogabulus

---

(1) Caligula, Roman Emperor, (37-41), sent cups of poison to his friends, ordered superannuated or sick gladiators, speculators or prisoners to be thrown to the wild beasts in the arena. When his terrible cruelties drove th people away from the ampitheatre, he closed the public granaries. One day, to express his displeasure at the applause in the circus, he exclaimed: "Would that Roman people had but one head, that I might cut it off with one stroke." He was shamelessly immoral.

(2) Nero, Roman Emperor, (54-68), procured the assassination of his own mother, sang verses and accompanied himself on the lyre, whilst watching the conflagration of Rome. When he was accused of having caused the fire he blamed it on the Christians. He ordered the first general persecution against them. Deserted by the people, abandoned even by the pretorians he ordered his grave to be dug; and gazing into it he exclaimed: "How great an artist is about to perish!" Finding no one who was willing to kill him, he stabbed himself.

(3) Domitian, Roman Emperor (81-96), the equal of any of his predecessors in obscenity, exceeded both Nero and Tiberius in cruelty; but, nevertheless, the Romans called him god, the son of Minerva. Pliny informs us that the streets leading to the Capitol were always bloody with the sacrifices of human victims before his statues. The career of this monster was cut short by his wife who induced one of his freedmen to kill him because he intended to proscribe her. Domitian decreed the second general persecution against the Christians.

(4) Commodus, Roman emperor (180-192), devoted much of his time to fighting and killing, in the public arena, opponents whose weapons were always blunt and edgeless, or cripples disguised as wild beasts. Such exhibitions regaled the frequenters of the Circus on seven hundred thirty-five occasions. After a reign of nearly thirteen years the wretch was poisoned by his closest attendants who had learnt he had ordered their death.

(5) Caracalla, Roman Emperor (211-217), committed excesses which defy description. In Rome alone, more than twenty thousand persons were executed under the pretext that they were partisans of Geta, brother of Caracalla, whom the latter had treacherously killed in his mother's arms. Caracalla was assasinated in his thirtieth year by Macrinus, prefect of the pretorians.

(*), etc., the people bowed before it without
resistance and without murmur, and from the
depths of their agony greeted the master with
the salutation of the dying gladiator. The
pagan world could think of no other form of
sovereign power, of no other manner of obey-
ing it.

It is worth noting that the jurists of the
Middle Ages, hypnotized by their *Corpus,* did
not recoil before the monstrous theory of
power so radically opposed to the Christian
principles and to the Germanic traditions.
Convinced of the ideal perfection of the Roman law, they did not see, or were not willing
to see, that undeniable defect of the masterpiece. Apparently they regarded imperial
absolutism, as the condition and the guaran-
tee of the perfection of the Roman law.
Doubtless they persudaded themselves that the
authority of the sovereign should be unlimited
in order to insure the full enforcement of
the law. Thus they accepted in its entirety
the judicial inheritance of the Roman
Empire; and Caesarism—which is the name
given in history to the Roman theory of ab-

(*) Heliogabalus, an oriental adventurer, a priest of the
Sun, (whence his name, Heliogabalus), became Roman emperor through the intrigues of his mother ,(218-222). During
the four years of rule his barbarity, immorality, and extrava-
gances exceeded those of any who had yet wielded the Roman
scepter. Among his ridiculous enactments we note his enroll-
ment of his grandmother among the Conscript Fathers.
Heliogabalus was killed by the pretorians.

solute power—became the first article of their political creed.

Nor is it surprising that men born in a free society should become the apologists of absolutism and dream of bringing mankind back to slavery. Similar aberrations are not uncommon; the plea of system explains them without justifying them. Moreover, men very seldom perceive the consequences of the principles they admit; and many would shudder at the practical application of principles which they have advocated with the greatest ardor. This is a natural infirmity of the human mind, which it may be humiliating to admit, but which it would be puerile to deny.

Kings of Germany strive to apply Caesarism.

When the jurists had sufficiently spread and developed their principles, there appeared sovereigns who were willing to apply them. They were the kings of Germany of the House of Suabia. The Hohenstaufen—a name derived from their paternal castle—had, moreover, great qualities of mind and, being possessed of boundless ambition, they became the ardent advocates of these doctrines whenever their thirst for power could profit by them. They were the first to put themselves forward as the legitimate and direct successors of the ancient Roman Emperors, in order that they might thus lay claim to all the power possessed by their assumed predecessors. Docile

pupils of the jurists, they found in their teachings inspiration for their political conduct and they endeavored to put their maxims into practice.

But the world of the Middle Ages was not yet ripe for slavery. The Papacy protested, the communes arose in opposition, a portion of feudalism itself refused to exchange a suzerain for a master. Emperor Frederic Barbarossa, in striving to impose on Italy laws dictated by the unmitigated spirit of Caesarism, encountered the stubborn resistance of the Lombard cities. In 1176, he was conquered by these at the celebrated battle of Legnano and compelled to recognize solemnly the rights he had trampled underfoot. His grandson, Frederick II, renewed the attempt in the thirteenth century; but, defeated in turn and excommunicated by the Pope, he was completely overthrown, and died in time to escape witnessing the fall and extermination of his whole dynasty.

Thus, on two successive occasions, the jurists were the losers of the game. On two successive occasions the Catholic spirit triumphed over the theories of Caesarism; and, on the ruins of an empire which the emperors themselves had destroyed by their ambition, the Catholic spirit kept intact the great principle of the Christian republic of the Middle Ages. Europe remained a moral and religious unit under the international magis-

tracy of peace intrusted to the Pope, who was
the protector of right and the guardian of
public liberties.

But, although in these two conflicts the nations had risen against the new idea, the idea
was not dead:—battles do not kill ideas. The
principles of Caesarism continued to spread
among the jurists, and their number increased
in a growing society which had more and
more need of them. Thus simultaneously in
all Europe there arose a caste of guiding
minds who were imbued with a system of
public law, anti-Christian in its essence, although often its adherents were themselves
not conscious of its anti-Christian character.
And the day came, half a century after their
second defeat, when the jurists at last had
their revenge.

Philip the Fair struggles for absolutism against Boniface VIII.

It was in France that they found their opportunity, and it was King Philip the Fair
who gave it to them. Grandson of Louis IX,
enjoying the prestige which the saintly king
had reflected upon his crown and dynasty,
himself one of the most tenacious and most
imperious characters known in history, Philip
the Fair had great power for either good or
evil. But unfortunately he was surrounded
by a group of jurists such as Enguerrand of
Marigny, Peter Flotte, William of Plaisians

William of Nogaret, whose society formed, in a way, his intellectual atmosphere. They imbued his mind with the new doctrine, and he emerged with the cold fanaticism of a despot, incapable of being stayed by a moral consideration and ready to sacrifice the whole universe to his ambition.

This man was to open a new phase of modern history. Indeed, his struggle against the Papacy is not merely an episode of the history of the Middle Ages, it is another turning point of universal history. Let us pause to consider the full importance of the struggle about to ensue.

When Pope Boniface VIII ascended the Pontifical throne (1294), sad events desolated Christendom. St. John of Acre, the last city held by the Christians in the Holy Land, had just been re-conquered by the Mohammedans. Thus all Palestine had fallen into their hands, and the blood shed in its defense by two million Christians had flown in vain during two centuries! It was a bitter sorrow for the Papacy, and Boniface VIII, in donning what Dante calls the weight of the great mantle, felt the sorrow in all its bitterness. His dream was to remedy this terrible situation by re-establishing peace among all the Christian princes and by obtaining from them a new expedition to the Holy Land. To bring this about it was absolutely necessary to prevent the war which seemed imminent between the King of France, Philip the Fair, and the King of England, Edward the First. This wicked war threatened to kindle a conflagration throughout all Europe. The two opponents secured allies on all sides: Philip counted on Scotland, Edward on the Empire, on Flanders, on Brabant. But, at this moment, true to the duty of his office, the Pope intervened to recall to sentiments of humanity those furious fools who, under the most futile pretexts, were preparing to deluge the world with blood. He spoke to them in words at once noble, firm, affectionate and hopeful, such as one would expect from the Chief of Christendom. "Are these," he said in substance, "exploits worthy of you and of your ancestors, and is it in this way that you fulfill your obligation of hastening to the assistance of the Christians of the Holy Land *"? Giving in to the entreaties of the Pope and perhaps also to the voice of their Christian conscience, the two rivals agreed to sign a truce of one year, which was to expire on June 24, 1296. It was an achievement full of promise for the cause of civilization, and so the Pope must have judged it, for, on April 13, 1296, of his own authority, he renewed the truce for a period of two years, and declared it obligatory

---

* Letter of May 28, 1295 in the Register of Boniface VIII., col. 295.

under pain of excommunication. However, in order to spare the self-love of the two kings and perhaps also because he had counted on their own spontaneous act, he had enjoined his legates to promulgate this truce only if the kings themselves did not take the initiative.[*]

Then was heard the voice of the King of France, striking, for the first time, a discordant note in the harmony of the social doctrine of the Middle Ages. Philip the Fair protested against the bull of the Pope; he refused even to listen to the reading of it before making the following declarations: "That the temporal government of his kingdom belonged to him alone; that in this matter he recognized no superior; that in this regard he would never submit to any living soul; that he wished to exercise his jurisdiction in his fiefs, defend his kingdom and pursue his right with the aid of his subjects, of his allies and of God; that the truce did not bind him. In matters spiritual, following the example of his predecessors, he was disposed to receive humbly the admonitions of the Holy See, like a true son of the Church."

He added that he accepted the mediation of the Pope, in the capacity of a private person and as a chosen arbiter, but in no way in the capacity of a recognized authority.

---

[*] Letters of the 16th and 17th of April 1296, in the Register of Boniface VIII, col. 59, et seq.

Declarations of Philip imply separation of politics and Christian morality.

Bear in mind the declarations of Philip the Fair; they have a wide bearing and go far beyond the question which provoked them. To deny to the Pope the right of intervening between belligerent kings in order to impose peace upon them meant more than the weakening of the most glorious and the most beneficent prerogative of the Holy See, more than the destruction of the only obstacle which prevented ambitious criminals from upsetting the world and deluging it with blood. However disastrous from this point of view were the declarations of the King of France for the future of European civilization, they were still more baneful because of the principle which inspired them. For the first time since the beginning of Christianity, they proclaimed the separation of politics and morality. The contrary had been recognized up to that time, and the kings themselves had admitted that their governments should conform to the moral law of Christianity. Philip the Fair denied this implicitly, since he was not willing that the will of the sovereign should be bound in the name of the law. This was tantamount to declaring that the royal power knew no limit, and, as a matter of fact, it no longer would have any other limits than those of its own choosing. It is the pagan theory in all its nakedness: *the prince is above the law; his will is the law. As the king wills, so wills the law.* And during five centuries it continued to be the axiom that inspired all governments.

It is well to note the origin of royal absolutism in Europe. We are at the antipodes of the Christian theory of power. The principles formulated by Philip the Fair were those which the Popes opposed and defeated in their twofold struggle against the Hohenstaufen; they were those which henceforth would be invoked whenever there was question of humiliating and belittling the Holy See, or whenever, despite the resistance of the Holy See, there was question of encroaching in one point or another upon the patrimony of Christian public right bequeathed the nations by former ages. And it is worthy of remark that a great number of historians, followed by a veritable mob of second-rate minds, persuade themselves with a naïveté almost ludicrous, that these theories of royal absolutism are Catholic theories. This is repeated to us every day in the polemics of the press, and I do not know what is more to be wondered at in the success of so bold a lie: the credulity of those who believe it or the audacity of those who circulate it.

Forbearance of Boniface VIII.

How did Pope Boniface VIII treat the declaration of the King of France, which accentuated with unrestrained crudity the violent opposition of the new politics to Catholic tradition? They who know this Pontiff only through the traditional lies of the State historiography, have a ready answer: "He protested, he manifested his indignation, he hurled the thunders of excommunication upon the head of the bold king of France." Not at all! Boniface VIII took the insult, let pass without protest the sophistries of the new politics, consented even to accept arbitration under the humiliating conditions imposed by the King of France: namely, not in the capacity of an authority and in the quality of Sovereign Pontiff, but in the role of a private person and—these are the exact words—"as Benedict Cajetan." * Why such condescension and forbearance? Apparently because, for the Pope, all other considerations gave way to the interest of public peace, even those considerations which concerned the dignity of the Holy See itself. Indeed, the Holy See, with an abnegation and a zeal which never failed for a single instant, devoted itself whole and entire to the great task of reconciling France and England. Notice, for example, how the Holy See addressed the German Emperor Adolph of Nassau, one of the enemies of Philip the Fair, in order to prevent him from taking up arms:

---

* This is the name of Boniface VIII previous to his elevation to the supreme Pontificate.

"We have passed sleepless nights, assuming voluntarily the burden, in order to be able to establish peaceful relations between you and our sons in Christ, the illustrious kings, Philip of France and Edward of England, and to secure tranquility to the Christian people, for the purpose of preventing the chiefs of the faithful and their subjects from turning against one another the swords which must be drawn in defense of the Holy Land and against the enemies of the Cross of Jesus Christ. And for this reason we warn you, we pray you, we exhort you earnestly and we entreat you, by the blood shed by Jesus Christ, not to attack the said King of France or his kingdom; but rather may your royal soul yield to our entreaties and be disposed to peace or at the very least to a long and sufficient truce, during which it will be possible to treat effectively of peace in our presence, through the envoys of the various parties."

At last, on June 27, 1298, Boniface VIII could render his sentence. It bore evidence of the purest equity, and certainly, as even French historians admit, it was not the King of France who had reason to complain. Indeed, the sentence approved the marriage of his daughter Isabella with the Prince of Wales, and through this union sacrificed the interests of the Count of Flanders, Guy of Dampierre, who had engaged in turn his two daughters to this prince and who saw them successively abandoned. But, as I have said already, in the eyes of the Pope, the cause of European peace led all other considerations. Finally, at the cost of many tribulations, he had obtained the result so ardently longed for, even though at the last moment the one who gained most from peace pretended that he hesitated to accept arbitration, as being too much to his disadvantage.

Characteristics of first encounter between Pope and King.

This was the first encounter between the Papacy and the new politics. I had to explain it in some detail, both because it is little known, and because it perfectly characterizes the attitudes of the two parties in the course of the long conflict which was about to open. The Papacy, as international magistracy and guardian of the general interests of Christendom, undertook to safeguard peace between the nations, and in order to attain this great result, made all sacrifices and concessions compatible with its high dignity. The King of France had no such concern. His only preoccupation was to establish his absolutism in spite of the sovereign Pontiff as well as of his own subjects, and without any regard for the general welfare of civilization. What concerned the Pope was the peace of the world; what concerned the King was his unlimited power. We should add—for it is of importance—that in this struggle the Pope represented the Catholic tradition of Europe, the King the revolutionary aspirations of the jurists. We note this opposition, however evident, because the hired forgers have here reversed the roles. In their version it was the Pope who innovated and it was the king who defended himself.

Philip the Fair attacks immunities of the Church.

The rest of the conflict between Boniface VIII and Philip the Fair presents the same characteristics as this first episode. The matter of ecclesiastical immunities, which broke out shortly afterwards, again brought in opposition the Papacy, which defended the traditional public right of Christian Europe, and the King, who sought to enthrone the revolutionary maxims of pagan rights. Philip was always in need of money, and his jurists had taught him that the possessions of his subjects belonged to him. Accordingly, he took whatever he could lay hands on. He took the possessions of the Knights Templars, he took the possessions of the Jews, he took the possessions of all the taxpayers by coining false money—it was natural that he should also wish to take the possessions of the Church.

But the possessions of the Church were protected by special immunities. In accordance with the doctrine of the time, they belonged

to the poor and they could not be taxed. This
did not mean, as some have asserted with in-
conceivable ignorance, that the Church did
not contribute to the public expenses. Far
from it! Only, it contributed in the form of
voluntary donations, by giving over to the
king, when he was in need of it, one tenth of
its entire revenue. This was called the tithes.
It has been calculated that in a little more
than half a century, from 1247 to 1300, the
French clergy paid to the king thirty-nine
tithes, almost four times its entire revenue, or
one-fifth of all its possessions. These figures
attest that the exemption from taxation was
for the Church a purely honorary privilege
and that the patriotism of the clergy neutral-
ized its immunities. Their *voluntary donations* were more burdensome than an obligatory tax would have been.

When, in 1295, the clergy were asked to pay
a new tithe, they protested and, upon repeated
and persistent demands, appealed to the
Pope. The Pope was the guardian of the
privileges of the entire Church and the protector of all her rights; when called upon by
the clergy of France, he was strictly bound,
under pain of failing in his most sacred obligations, to come to the rescue of the op-
pressed, and he did. I shall not relate the
varying fortunes of this new conflict with
the crown. It will suffice to state that here
again the Pope showed the greatest forbear-

ance towards the prevaricating King. The Pope recalled to the mind of the King, as was his duty, that he had no right to impose taxes upon the clergy without the consent of the Pope, but he assured the King that he would never refuse his consent whenever there would be question of the defense of the kingdom and that he would sell the sacred treasures rather than endanger so great a cause. He added that in case of urgent and very evident necessity, he would even permit that they should proceed without awaiting his consent, but that, in all other cases, they should submit to the law. One must admit that this was pushing the spirit of conciliation as far as justice permitted, and, thanks to the moderation of both, the conflict was once more avoided.

Philip attacks Pope's ambassador.

But peace was to be short-lived. Contempt of law was always the characteristic trait of Philip the Fair; he did not seem to enjoy the fulness of the royal prerogative so long as he encountered any limits to his power. One day the Pope sent a messenger to ask for the release of the unfortunate Count of Flanders, Guy of Dampierre, who was languishing in the prisons of the King. The ambassador, who was entrusted with a message so worthy of the Father of the faithful, was Bernard Saisset, Bishop of Pamiers. What took place in the interview between the King and the

Bishop? We do not know, but the King pretended that the ambassador had used language that was not respectful, and he pursued
the unfortunate prelate with incredible
rancor. He demanded that the Pope should
take from him his episcopal charter and even
the privilege of clerical immunity (*), in
order that he himself might afterwards im-
peach him before a lay tribunal and have him
condemned as a State criminal. This demand
was a veritable mockery. One might say that
the King was jesting in exacting of the Pope,
at one and the same time, the violation of all
the most sacred rights: the respect due to a
bishop, the lawful immunity of the priest, the
sacred character of the ambassador, not to
speak of the ignominy in imposing upon the
Pope such odious measures against his legate
whose only crime was that he had served his
master!

The Pope replied with calm dignity and
fortitude; he called up the cause of Bernard Saisset at this own tribunal, and he took
steps to convene a council in Rome to adopt
measures to meet the situation. At the
same time he addressed the tyrant himself in
the bull *Ausculta fili,* where he set forth his
grievances. The tone of the document is dis-

_____

(*) Clerical Immunity, as recognized by the Christian
States in the Middle Ages, withdrew the clergy from secular
jurisdiction, so that not only spiritual lawsuits of clerics, but
also temporal lawsuits, whether criminal or civil, fell exclusively within the jurisdiction of ecclesiastical judges.

closed by its very title *(Listen, my son).* To
these legitimate measures, the King, prompted
by his jurists, replied with unheard-of violence and deceit. He convened the States-
General of France, and read to them a false
papal bull which had been made up by his
men of law, in which they put haughty and
scornful language into the mouth of the Sovereign Pontiff, ordered a jurist to read a
reply to the Pope which was a tissue of revolting calumnies, and, as a result of these
infamous maneuvers, he obtained from the
deceived and terrorized States-General a bill
of indemnity for his conduct towards the
Pope.

Philip causes arrest of Pope.

This time the cup of patience was full to
overflowing. The Pope fulminated the bull
Unam Sanctam, a solemn and moderate expo-
sition of the pure Catholic doctrine on the
relations between the two powers, in accordance with the tradition of the Church, such as
might have been formulated by Gregory VII,
Alexander III (1) or Innocent III (2). At

---

(1) Alexander III, Pope, (1159-81), foremost as a
canonist, and ecclesiastical legislator and a valiant defender
of the rights of the Church against the encroachments of
kings and emperors; he overcame the violence of the Emperor Barbarossa and compelled Henry II of England to
ask pardon for the murder of Thomas Becket.

(2) Innocent III, one of the greatest popes of the
Middle Ages (1161-1216) was a learned theologian and one
of the greatest jurists of his time and a strenuous defender
of the rights of the Church. He steadily strove to put an end
to hostilities among Christian princes. He prepared a crusade against the Moors. He undertook the Fourth Crusade.
He extended his beneficent influence practically over the
whole Christian world.

the same time, he prepared the excommunication of the prevaricating King. Then Philip
the Fair decided to make his final stroke.
Surpassing all his past crimes, he dispatched
to Italy one of the vilest insulters of the Pope,
William of Nogaret, with the mission to insti-
gate a plot against the Holy See. The wretch,
after having endeavored to shake the fidelity
of the Roman people, set out for Anagni with
the intention of surprising the old man in his
little town. Boniface was without defense.
He donned his pontifical insignia, and, holding in his hand the keys of St. Peter, awaited
his enemies. Neither this grandeur of soul,
nor the majesty of the Vicar of Jesus Christ,
nor the white hair of a man of eighty-six years,
moved the criminals. The Pope remained in
their power for three days; the third day the
inhabitants of Anagni rose in opposition and
drove them out. Boniface did not wish that
they should be pursued, but so many emotions
had broken his strength and a few days afterwards he expired.

Great was the indignation of the Christian
world on hearing of the attempt made at
Anagni. Dante, despite his supposed grievance against the venerable Pope, has forever
branded the contemptible authors of the das-
tardly assault in these immortal verses: "I
see the fleurs de lis enter Anagni, I see the
Christ imprisoned in His Vicar, I see Him
again given over to derision, I see Him again

drenched with vinegar and gall, and crucified between new thieves. *

Philip attacks memory of Boniface.

This judgment of the greatest poet of the
Middle Ages is also the honest judgment of
humanity, and the cowardly courtiers of royal
absolutism were not unaware of it; accordingly, following the example of the royal mal-
efactor, they worked with boundless fury and
cynicism to pervert the opinion of posterity.
After having outraged their victim, they
wished to disgrace him; after having grieved
him to death, they attempted to dishonor
his name. It would be difficult to form an
idea of the intense rancor with which Philip
the Fair strove to bring into contempt the
memory of Boniface VIII with his successors: he was foiled in his attempt, but the diversion was cleverly made to turn attention
away from his own crimes and, in this at
least, he succeeded. As to the official histori-
ographers, especially such as Dupuy, Baillet
and others, they continued the tradition
bequeathed them by the jurists of Philip
the Fair. They fabricated some documents; they falsified others; when they
could neither destroy nor alter, they at
least changed the dates, to modify their
bearing and often to make them express

---

* **Dante, Purgatorio, XX. 86-90.**

a contrary meaning; in a word, they
have heaped upon the memory of Boniface
VIII such a load of lies and calumnies, that
after five centuries we have not yet succeeded in clearing entirely the field of history.

Modern French historians exonerate Boniface.

Nevertheless the hour of justice has struck.
Now that royal absolutism, defeated in turn,
no longer has at its service the corrupt pens
of its flatterers, the French historians themselves to-day admit to what extent their kings
made travesty of truth at a time when it was
to their profit to disfigure it.   They admit,
too, that, in this resounding drama, the ag-
gression came not from the Papacy, which was
content with defending its traditional position,
but from the royal power, which, armed with
the theories of Caesarism, sought the overthrow of a political regime which was based
on the religious unity of the world and on the
indirect power of the Sovereign Pontiffs.
"Boniface VIII," writes Mr. Boutaric in a
celebrated book, "did not bring new pretensions to the See of Peter: his politics towards
outside princes were those of his predecessors *". But no one will contend that the
politics of Philip the Fair were those of St.
Louis: they were, at the most, those of Fred-

---

* E. Boutaric, La France sous Philippe le Bel, p. 94.

erick of Suabia, and these, in last analysis,
were the politics of the Roman Caesars. In
other words, they were pagan politics, making
a fresh effort to take the guidance of these
modern states away from Christian principles.

I have already stated that these politics
have triumphed and I have indicated, in the
beginning of this lecture, what connivances
they found at an early hour in the social body.
In conclusion I wish to indicate briefly the
results of their victory.

Evil results of neo-Caesarism.

It was, first of all, the destruction of what
has been called the Christian Republic of the
Middle Ages. Up to then Europe was strongly
united not only by the identity of religious
beliefs but also by the identity of political
maxims. It connected public right with
Christian morality, and recognized as the in-
terpreter of the latter the Vicar of Jesus
Christ. From the time of Philip the Fair it
was so no more. There was no longer a
Christian Republic, as was evidenced by the
disappearance of what was its wonderful
manifestation—the Crusades. St. Louis had
been the last of the Christian kings, he was
also the last of the Crusaders. And Europe,
which up to that time had carried the standard of the Cross to Jerusalem, to Tunis, to
Damascus, recoiled before the Crescent. They

had to give back Jerusalem and hand over Constantinople to Islam. Mohammed became again the arbiter of the Mediterranean and the Turks the terror of the world. We can blame neo-Caesarism for plunging the most beautiful lands of the earth into barbarism. Behold, from an international point of view, the balance sheet of royal absolutism!

From a national point of view the absolutism of kings has broken the equilibrium of the social body, concentrated all the life in the head, atrophied free institutions and made revolution the only possible corrective of tyranny. Nor is that all. The Christian nations wrenched from the guidance of the Church have not found their way; they seem condemned to travel the whole cycle of error before finding their way again. Ever and anon they turn to new systems which become bankrupt one after another. Philosophism, liberalism, socialism, anarchism, to say nothing of the intermediate doctrines, are the legitimate heirs of royal absolutism; like it, they will betray their promises. The unrest will last as long as the destiny of the Christian nations remains in the hands of a political system which does not worry about Christian principles. The Catholic Church, seated at the foot of the Cross, waits calmly for the day when revolution shall have finished the

education of mankind. (*)

* At this point it is refreshing to note how Pope Benedict XV, from the day of his coronation, did not cease to entreat the belligerent nations to make a just and durable peace, how, in particular, on August 1, 1917, in a letter addressed to the leaders of all the belligerent peoples, compelled by a sentiment of his supreme duty as the common father of the faithful, in the name of the Divine Redeemer, the Prince of Peace, he admonished them to reflect on their very grave responsibility before God and before man, begged them to substitute for the material force of arms the moral force of right, to adopt compulsory arbitration of all national questions in order to reach a just and durable peace.

In harmony with the above President Wilson in his address to Congress, February 11, 1918, made the following striking declarations:

"What we are striving for is a new international order based upon broad and universal principles of right and justice . . . .

"Each part of the final settlement must be based on justice . . . .

"We believe that our own desire for a new international order, under which reason and justice and the common interests of mankind shall prevail, is the desire of enlightened men everywhere . . . .

"Having set our hand to the task of achieving it, we shall not turn back."

On September 6, 1924, at Geneva, the Fifth Assembly of the League of Nations, in which forty-six of the fifty-four nation members participated, unanimously adopted a resolution for the study by the Disarmament Commission of changes in the League Covenant and the Permanent Court of International Justice protocol to promote disarmament and compulsory arbitration, with a view to an early conference of nations.

The un-official American representatives at Geneva, made the following statement: "There is a spirit in the discussions and purposes of the countries represented here which gives every promise for the future of the world."

Whilst the Church is weeping at the foot of the cross upon which erring mankind is crucified, may we not see in these statements of Pope and President and in the resolution of the Fifth Assembly of the League of Nations and the statement of the American representatives the dawn of the better day for which Christendom is calmly waiting?

The Church and the Renaissance

The Renaissance is a natural development of society of Middle Ages.

The Renaissance is, unquestionably, one of the most remarkable phenomena in the history of humanity. At the outset it is well to note that the term *Renaissance or Revival of learning* is a misnomer for the vast intellectual movement of the fifteenth and sixteenth centuries. What really took place was not so much a revival of learning as a flowering out of the learning of preceding centuries. It is a capital error to hold that this epoch marks an abrupt and sudden resurrection of intellectual life after long centuries of darkness. In history, as in nature, there can be no effect without a cause. From nothing comes nothing; all things are bound together by the law of cause and effect. The movement of the Renaissance was in keeping with the laws of accelerated motion: it was but the natural, progressive and uninterrupted development of the society of the Middle Ages unfolding from century to century down to the opening of the present age. Modern genius had for parent the society of the Middle Ages and grew up with it during the laborious and fruitful centuries

of its infancy; finally, it reached the heyday
of youth when, like an opening flower, it dis-
closed suddenly all its rich and magnificent
vitality.

This view of the Renaissance is in keeping
with all the laws of nature and all the teachings of history. As Pascal, the well-known
French philosopher, remarks, *"The whole succession of men should be considered as
one man who lives on and never ceases to
learn."*. This is especially true of modern
society. From the days of Charlemagne down
to the sixteenth century, modern society had
not ceased to develop its acquired knowledge
and increase its intellectual capital. On a
certain day it found itself rich without being
able to mark the precise moment when its
poverty had changed into wealth. Nothing
would be more interesting than to study the
different phases of this intellectual progress
as they succeeded one another in the course
of the ages, such as the revival under Charlemagne—the development of modern languages—the progress of these languages
alongside of the scientific language—the
birth of popular poetry and the great
epics—the appearance of the poetry of love
and chivalry—the troubadours and the *minnesingers*—the theater with its original setting—the great philosophical and theological
discussions of the twelfth century—the advent of experimental science with Roger

Bacon (1)—the vast intellectual movement created by the powerful impulse of the Crusades—the elaboration of the encyclopedias in which such geniuses as Thomas of Aquin, Albert the Great (2), and such compilers as Vincent of Beauvais (3) summarized the knowledge of their times—the splendor of the plastic arts which covered all Europe with unequaled monuments— the great voyages of exploration which, from the beginning of the sixteenth century, opened up a new and strange horizon by advancing beyond the circle of existing knowledge—and then the inventions which hastened the march of progress and made new advances possible to mankind.

A few examples will illustrate ⁿ meaning. The fact that Christopher Columbus discov-

(1) Roger Bacon, English philosopher, born 1214; died at Oxford, perhaps June 11, 1294. He must be reckoned among the most eminent scholars of all time. His chief work is the "Opus Maius," composed at the request of Pope Clement IV. It is a general treatise on the sciences.

(2) Albert the Great, scientist, philosopher, and theologian, born about 1206 in Swabia; died at Cologne, November 15, 1280. He is called "the Great," and "Universal Doctor," in recognition of his extraordinary genius and extensive knowledge. He was proficient in every branch of learning cultivated in his day ,and surpassed all his contemporaries, except perhaps Roger Bacon (1214-94), in the knowledge of nature. He was a priest of the Dominican Order. He was beatified in 1622, and the Bishops of Germany, in 1872, sent to the Holy See a petition for his canonization.

(3) Vincent of Beauvais, undertook a systematic and comprehensive treatment of all branches of human knowledge in his great work: "Speculum Majus." This book treats of theology, philosophy, natural sciences, medicine, surgery, jurisprudence, history and literature. The "Speculum Majus" contains 80 books divided into 9885 chapters, figures which give some idea of the magnitude of the work accomplished by the Dominican priest in the first half of the thirteenth century.

ered the West Indies and Vasco da Gama the East Indies does not signify that these two explorers were wonderful initiators who, appearing like meteors, drew humanity after them into fields hitherto unexplored. No! They were the heirs of those intrepid Portuguese navigators who, in a series of voyages that had extended over more than a century, had explored the entire coast of Western Africa as far as the mouth of the Congo, leaving to their successors the task of finishing the work and appropriating all the glory. In like manner when Gutenberg discovered the art of multiplying the works which contained the best that human genius had produced, he was but applying in an ingenious manner the ideas of the monks who, many centuries before, consecrated their lives to copying manuscripts, "piercing the devil with as many strokes as they traced characters upon paper." Gutenberg was the immediate successor—the intellectual heir—of those *Brothers of the pen* who had thought out the solution of the same problem by making themselves, so to speak, living writing-machines.

It would be easy to continue this review, for everywhere we cannot but notice that existing capital is always abundantly productive and that, at a given moment, there results inevitably an enormous increase of social wealth. This intellectual phenomenon of the

sixteenth century is similar to the economic
phenomenon witnessed at the beginning of
the nineteenth century, when machinery mul-
tiplied production indefinitely and threw
upon the markets, for the use of all, an in-
calculable quantity of industrial products.
Just as the discovery of machinery was made
possible only by reason of the vast conquests
of the natural sciences, dating from the sixteenth century, so in like manner the conquests of the sixteenth century were prepared
and worked out by the sustained and constant
efforts of the generations of the Middle Ages.
The intellectual life of the world at that time
may be likened to the top of a ladder, each
rung of which was occupied by a generation.
The luscious fruits which ripen on the tree
of civilization are the last results of an in-
numerable series of patient and disinterested
efforts; they represent the succession of
generations that have disappeared.

Such being the true view of the Renaissance, it is amusing to read the contention of
many writers that this imposing phenomenon
was due to the fact that Greek professors,
driven from the Orient by the Turkish invasions, happened to bring to amazed Western
Europe the literary treasures of antiquity.
These treasures of antiquity were in possession of Western Europe before the coming
of the professors; from the professors
it took but a small part of these

treasures at a time when, by its own efforts, it
had become capable of appreciating them.
The revival of ancient literature in Western
Europe is a consequence, not the origin, of
the Renaissance.

**The Renaissance leads some to imitate morals of pagan
antiquity.**

But all wealth—material or intellectual—
has its dangers. Material riches enervate the
heart by voluptuousness, intellectual riches
puff up the mind with pride. And when
the Gospel says: "Woe to the rich!", we may
believe that these hard words apply not only
to those who bend under the load of gold but
also to those who succumb beneath the weight
of knowledge. Neither the one nor the other
can enter the Kingdom of God, if they are not
poor in spirit, that is, if they do not use their
treasures for the higher ends of charity. And
I am convinced that it was especially to those
who have attained the heights of intellectual
life that the Lord wished to teach a lesson
when He placed a child in the midst of His
disciples and declared that heaven is closed
to those who are not like unto that little one.

Now, it was to this danger, inherent in all
riches and which consists in loving riches for
themselves, that many men of this epoch suc-
cumbed. I do not speak of those who became
attached to material wealth and to the sensual
enjoyments it procures; the voluptuaries do
not count in history, their social action is null,

they represent the purely negative element in
the destinies of humanity. Here we are concerned with those who, in modern parlance,
are called the *intellectuals*—those who assimu-
lated all the culture of their times and reacted on the minds of their contemporaries.
For many of these intellectual life had the
effect of an intoxicant: it inebriated them.
They knew no measure in their enjoyment.
They refused to heed the moral law of moderation. They would be humanists above all
else, they were not much concerned about remaining Christians. Like the jurists of the
twelfth century they gave themselves body
and soul to the worship of antiquity. They
were pagans because the ancients were pagans
and, according to the energetic expression
of Holy Writ, they became like to their idol.

Does this mean that one may not study
antiquity without succumbing to its spell,
without becoming pagan in mind and heart?
Far from it! We have instances to the contrary. The Carolingian revival remained
thoroughly Christian in inspiration, notwithstanding the preponderant part it gave to
ancient literature; and the powerful geniuses
of the thirteenth century, although mainly
nourished by antiquity, borrowed from it
only its beneficent elements and remained conscious of their own superiority. St. Thomas of
Aquin has not enslaved modern thought to the
philosophy of his master Aristotle; rather,

he made Aristotle contribute to the demonstration of Christian truth.   Dante Alighieri
was devoted to Virgil and saw in him the
personification of human knowledge, but he
surpassed Virgil in that he loved Beatrice,
the symbol of divine knowledge.   These are
illustrious models from whom the men of the
fifteenth and sixteenth centuries might have
drawn inspiration.   In fact, there were a
great number among the humanists of that
time whom literature did not turn from Christianity; among others were Rudolph Agricola
(1), Vittorino da Feltre (2), Aleandro (3), Maffeo Vegio (4), Sadoleto (5), Vida (6), Pico della

---

(1) Rudolph Agricola, (Huysmann) born in Holland
about 1443, died at Heidelberg, Germany, 1485. He was re-
nowned for the study of the ancients, the elegance of his
Latin style, his knowledge of philosophy, Hebrew and Scripture. He zealously promoted the study of classics in Germany. He was deeply religious.

(2) Vittorino De Rambaldoni da Feltre, born at Feltre Italy,
in 1378; died 1446. He strove to create the perfect school.
He taught Greek and Latin literature, philosophy, mathematics, etc. He gave his students plenty of physical exercise
in the shape of wrestling, racing, riding, and dancing. He
made the rich pay for the poor.

(3) Aleandro Girolamo (1480-1542) a humanist. He
went to Paris in 1508, gave lectures in Greek, Latin and
Hebrew and was made rector of the university. Later he became papal nuncio in Germany to deal with Luther's case.
He was created archbishop of Brindisi, Italy, and cardinal.

(4) Maffeo, Veggio (1406-1458), poet; wrote on education.

(5) Sadoleto, Jacopo, cardinal, humanist and reformer,
born at Modena, Italy, 1477; died at Rome 1547. He was
versed in the various branches of Latin and Italian culture.
He was secretary to Leo X. In 1517 he was appointed bishop
of Carpentras, near Avignon, France. Unlike many of the
humanists, he was a man of blameless life and attentive to
all his duties as a priest and bishop. As poet, orator, theologian, and philosopher he was in the foremost rank of his
time.

(6) Vida, Marco Girolami, humanist, born at Cremona,
Italy, about 1490; died in 1566. He is the author of a great
Christian epic, "Christias." He also wrote, "De Arte Poetica,"
inspired by the ancient Roman writer Quintilian. Vida's
style is clear, elegant, harmonious and ordinarily simple.

Mirandola (1), Alexander Hegius (2), Thomas More (3), Cardinal Fisher (4), Louis

(1) **Mirandola, Giovanni Pico della,** Italian philosopher and scholar, born 1463; died 1494. He devoted himself to the study of philosophy and theology, Greek, Latin, Syriac, and Arabic. Towards the end of his life he destroyed his poetical works, gave up profane science and determined to give his time to the defense of Christianity against Jews, Mohammedans, and Astrologers. Savonarola delivered his funeral oration.

(2) **Alexander Hegius,** humanist; born probably in 1433, at Heeck, Westphalia; died 1498. He was ordained a priest when of quite mature age. He spoke and wrote a pure Ciceronian Latin, and was equally versed in Greek. He established a school for the study of these languages in Holland and simplified and improved the method of teaching.

(3) **Thomas More,** Blessed, knight, lord chancellor of England, author and martyr, born in London about 1477, executed at Tower Hill, Judy 6, 1535. He studied at Oxford, mastered the Greek and Latin languages, French, history, mathematics, and law; was made lecturer on law; wrote poetry, both Latin and English; cultivated the acquaintance of learned men, of Erasmus, among others. Besides law and the classics he read the writings of the ancient Fathers. For some time he considered the question of becoming a priest. He decided to practice law, in which profession he scored immediate success. On July 1, 1535 More was indicted for high treason at Westminster Hall before a special commission of twenty, on the charge of denying Parliament's power to confer ecclesiastical supremacy on Henry VIII. He was found guilty, sentenced to death, and executed five days later. Blessed Thomas More was formally beatified by Pope Leo XIII., December 26, 1886. Of all his writings the most famous is the "Utopia."

(4) **John Fisher,** Blessed, cardinal, Bishop of Rochester, and martyr; born at Beverly, Yorkshire, England, 1459; died June 22, 1535. At Cambridge he received successively the degrees of B. A. in 1487, M. A. in 1491, D. D. in 1501, was elected Vice-Chancellor in 1501, Chancellor in 1504, to which post he was re-elected annually for ten years and then appointed for life. Besides his share in the Lady Margaret's foundations, Fisher gave further proof of his genuine zeal for learning by inducing Erasmus to visit Cambridge. He is the author of twenty-six works in all, several of which have been reprinted several times. He denied the spiritual supremacy of the king; opposed openly the divorce of Henry VIII and Catherine of Aragon and refused to acknowledge the legitimacy of the offspring of Henry VIII and Anna Boleyn. He was sent to the tower of London April 26, 1534, sentenced to death and executed. He was formally beatified by Pope Leo XIII in 1886

Vives (1), our own admirable Cleynaerts (2).

But we must admit that all minds have not the same degree of virtue or of intellectual health. Many fell victims to the poisonous perfume which issued from the tomb of antiquity. They were not startled by the vices which Christian morality reproves, when these vices were idealized and surrounded with all the prestige of poetry. They envied the absolute liberty of ancient thought which, free from the fetters of truth, wandered at will in the boundless field of philosophic speculation. Often, unwittingly, they were drawn away from the sure positions which Christian education had secured for mind and heart. They lowered the water-mark of morality to bring it down to the level of antiquity; they let go the truths which they

---

(1)   Vives, Juan Luis, Spanish humanist and philosopher, born at Valencia in 1492; died at Bruges, Belgium, May 6, 1540.   He first studied at the University of Paris, 1519, was appointed professor at the University of Louvain, where he was associated with Erasmus; in 1523 he became attached to the Corpus Christi College, Oxford, was banished from England for opposing the divorce of Henry VIII.   He is the author of numerous works of great merit and popularity, on Christian piety, teaching and education, political economy and philosophy.   He also showed himself an organizer of public relief.

(2)   Cleynaerts, Belgian Priest, and Orientalist.   His thorough knowledge of the Hebrew and Arabic languages, literature and history led him to advocate preaching to the Jews and the Mohammedans rather than fighting them with the sword.   He strove to establish at Louvain, a seminary for training priests for missionary work among Mohammedans. He spent some months in Africa evangelizing the followers of Mohammed.   He died in Granada, Spain.

thought enchained them but which in reality sustained them.

The result was inevitable. The hope that they might keep themselves intact with imaginations so infatuated was as vain as the pretensions of certain young men of our time who, under pretext of literary studies, ask of their confessor permission to read all the productions of the pornographic writers of our day, believing that they can escape from such association with unsullied imagination, sound moral judgment, unswerving will! Thus the passionate study of the Greeks and Romans produced on the different classes of admirers various phenomena. We shall classify these phenomena and then strive to estimate them at their true value.

The Renaissance leads all to exaggerate literary merits of pagan antiquity.

In the sixteenth century everyone—the best Christians as well as the most pronounced pagans—fell with exemplary docility under the literary charm of antiquity. We may call this the *minimum* of pagan influence. It was the universal conviction that the ancients had conceived types of the beautiful which could never be equaled, and that we moderns have to imitate these types unvaryingly, if we wish in turn to realize an esthetic ideal. No one doubted that the ancients had created the moulds into which we must cast the produc-

tions of our own genius if we would escape
the penalty of producing barbarous and monstrous works; and that our highest artistic
effort was to imitate the ancients and thus to
reach the perfection of the works which they
had drawn from their imagination. It was
irrevocably decreed that the role of creator
was reserved to antiquity and that the modern
age must content itself with the character of
imitator.

This odd conception of esthetic life is ex
plained in great measure by the ignorance of
those who formulated it. For a long time
past the Middle Ages had ceased to be known,
nor were they to be known again for a long
time to come. The judgments of Boileau, in
his *Art Poétique,* are very significant in this
respect. He was convinced—and he expresses
his conviction with delightful assurance—that
our devout forefathers knew no kind of poetry, were ignorant of rythm, and were
without the pleasures of the theatre. These
assertions will appear absurd to him who
knows that the Troubadours (1) and the Minnesingers (2) of the Middle Ages are the

---

(1) Troubadours, lyrical poets who flourished from the
eleventh to the latter part of the thirteenth century, princi-
pally in southern France, Catalonia, Aragon, and northern
Italy. Their poetry was characterized by an almost exclusive
devotion to the subject of chivalric love.

(2) Minnesingers were German lyric poets and singers
of the twelfth and thirteenth centuries, so called because love
was the chief theme of their poems.

fathers of modern lyric poetry, that from that
period date all our epics—the incomparable
Chanson de Roland (1), *the Poem of the
Cid* (2), *the Nibelungenlied* (3), *the Roman du Renard* (4),—that the theatre never
enjoyed greater popularity nor exerted a
greater social influence than in the Middle
Ages. No wonder that in our own day Littré
lectures good Nicholas Despréaux Boileau
and suggests that his judgments are, hardly
worthy of the author of the "Art Poétique."

But there is something more than ignorance

---

(1)   Chanson de Roland, a French epic, put into writing
about the year 1080, and by an unknown author, is the most
celebrated of the history songs of the Middle Ages. It is
the story of the death of Roland at Roncevalles and Charlemagne's vengeance. It places vividly before the imagination
the France of those times, warlike, violent, but fairly ani-
mated with an ardent faith. It has recently been done into
English, in the original measure, by Mr. Charles Scott
Moncrieff, under the title, "The Song of Roland.".—Chapman
and Hall, London.

(2)   Poem of the Cid or Romances of the Cid, a Spanish
poem composed by an unknown author about A. D. 1200. The
Cid is the principal national hero of Spain, famous for his
exploits in the wars with the Moors. The poem is a spirited
exhibition of national peculiarities in the chivalrous times
of Spain.

(3)   Nibelungenlied or Song of Nibelungen, a Middle
High German epic, the greatest monument of early German
in the first half of the thirteenth century. The Nibelungen,
in the German legend, were a race of Northern dwarfs, conquered by the mythological hero, Siegfried.

(4)   The "Roman du Renard" is a vast collection, formed
early in the thirteenth century, of stories in verse thrown
together without sequence or connection. In all its parts the
same hero appears again and again, "Renard" the fox. The
action round about Renard is carried on by many other characters, such as the wolf, the lion, the cock, pseudo-animals
that mingle with their bearing and instinct as animals,
traits and feelings borrowed from humanity. It is a kind of
parody of the "history songs." It ridicules the nobles, feudal
society and feudal institutions.

in the literary view of the people of the sixteenth and seventeenth centuries: there is a
real infatuation. It was, alas, at that time
that good Father Maffei sought permission to
read his Breviary in Greek, that his style
might not be spoiled by the bad Latin of the
Church. It was at that time that Ferreri,
who had been intrusted by Leo X with the
reform of the Latin Breviary, disfigured its
most beautiful hymns under pretext of removing its barbarisms, treated the Blessed
Virgin as a nymph and a goddess, and spoke
of God as the sovereign of the gods. And
what are we to say of the prejudices regarding plastic art! Men who lived and died under the shadow of our marvelous Gothic
cathedrals disfigured these noble monuments
to make them look like the Greek temples with
their feeble and cold beauty. They had under
their eyes the radiant majesty of the portals
of Rheims, of Paris and of Amiens—and they
despised them! One of the most enlightened
and, certainly, one of the most sympathetic
of the great writers of the seventeenth century—our good Fénelon—formulated against
the art of our fathers a condemnation whose
every line and whose every word is an outrage
against truth, good taste and esthetic sense.
This strange blindness can find explanation
only in the *a priori* conviction that there is
no beauty except in ancient art and in
its imitations: the absolute artistic superi-

ority of the ancients was an axiom as incontestable as the dogmas of the Christian faith.

Infatuation with pagan antiquity begets in some contempt for Christianity.

In vain would one have tried to make these persons understand that they were injuring Christianity in considering it incapable of attaining an ideal of beauty; they would have replied to you with Boileau:

De la religion les mystères terribles
D'ornements égayés ne sont pas susceptibles. *

And if one had urged the matter further, they would have declared that there is nothing in common between religion and esthetics —very much as in our own day, in our own country (Belgium), some members of the Right say there is nothing in common between religion and economic questions, while members of the Left say that there is nothing in common between religion and politics.

Who does not see that already there was, even among the best, a real diminution of the Christian faith, since they excluded its influence from the whole vast intellectual domain, dividing their minds into two compartments —one reserved to art and poetry, the other to religion. They did not know, or they had lost sight of the fact, that Christianity is like the

---

* "The awful mysteries of religion are not susceptible of cheerful ornaments."

sun which must penetrate everything to vivify
everything; that there is such a thing as
Christian esthetics just as there is Christian
politics and Christian economics; that the
beautiful, like the true and the good, is one
of the aspects of the Supreme Being, God;
and that, in art as in nature, nothing is beautiful which does not bear on its brow the reflection of the uncreated Beauty. It seems
that in those days no one suspected these
truths which are an integral part of Christian doctrine; they had to await the *Genius of
Christianity* by Chateaubriand to be reminded
of the fact that the Catholic religion possesses
some beauty.

Imbued with such veneration for ancient
literature, how could one keep himself free
from a like infatuation for the civilization of
which this literature was the expression? For
the genius of ancient literature with seductive
eloquence and poetic beauty depicted the
ancient world in a radiant and almost divine
light. And the men of the Renaissance, view-
ing it through a halo, pictured to themselves
an antiquity which had never existed, an
antiquity where everything was beautiful and
grand, luminous and serene, where nobility of
heart went side by side with largeness of
mind, an antiquity where all things human
took on more than natural proportions, where
the historic heroes had the gait of demi-gods,
and from which emerged sages, walking with

their disciples in the shade of the Grove of Academus (1), discussing the existence of God and the immortality of the soul. Thus the Christian imagination of the men of the Renaissance projected its own mental image on the clouds which veiled the past and, without knowing it, admired itself in a world which was nothing but its own reflection.

But it may be objected that there is no great harm in all this and that we have here but one of those ever recurring illusions which will never cease to baffle men. But this contention will hardly hold, for I notice that all who have professed this enthusiastic veneration for the ancients have been correspondingly unjust towards Christian society and Christianity. If it were true that the most noble representatives of the human race are found among the pagans, if it were true, as Thiers (2) stated in an official report, "that antiquity is the most beautiful thing in the world", then, to be logical, one would have to say with the poet:

"No need there were for Mary to give birth." (3)

--- --- ---

(1)   The Grove of Academus was the resort where Plato, the great Greek philosopher taught for nearly fifty years, till his death in 348 B. C.

(2)   Thiers, Louis Adolphe (1797-1877) French journalist, statesman and historian.

(3)   Mestier non era partorir Maria.   (Dante, Purgatorio, III, 39.)

In other words Christianity would be useless—nay more—it would be responsible for
the decadence of humanity, if since its advent
mankind had lost all that constitutes true
genius. Christianity would have been but an
empty parenthesis: by closing the parenthesis
and returning to the sources of antiquity, the
human mind would find itself again and re-
sume the interrupted course of its glorious
destinies.

Some admirers of the Renaissance attempt to paganize
the modern world.

This conclusion was so logical that it soon
found some who had the courage to deduce it.
In contradistinction of those naïve persons
who Christianized antiquity, they would paganize the modern world—and they began the
experiment with themselves. They took from
antiquity its manner of thinking and its way
of living. Shaking from their minds the yoke
of dogma and from their hearts the burden
of the moral law, they undertook to use, as
they liked, the powerful faculties of thinking
and of willing which belong to man and whose
use providential laws have at all times regulated. They wantonly stripped themselves of
the twofold superiority which they owed to
Christianity, and rejoiced in descending again
to the level of pagan naturalism, where grace
was absent. They forgot the origin of man,
they forgot, above all, his last end; they aban-

doned that narrow road by which the Master wished us to enter into eternal life; they took the broad way of living, which knows neither the joys of sacrifice freely accepted, nor the consolations of sorrow borne with resignation, nor the sublime delights of charity which raises man up to God. For them, as for the ancients, their whole existence was centered on voluptuousness and glory—this was their twofold ideal of life.

Of voluptuousness I shall not speak, except to state that no ancient was exempt from its defilements, that the most celebrated men of antiquity, even when they triumphed over their senses, mastered them for the time only, to succumb to them later. There did not exist among the pagans a soul truly proof against voluptuousness, and, if one were found, the exception would but prove the rule.

Love of glory is no doubt a more elevated sentiment, and at times we find in antiquity examples of it which command our respect. I know of no more beautiful instance of it than the words spoken by the dying Epaminondas in reply to those who lamented that he left no children to inherit his glory: "Friends, I die content; I leave two immortal daughters, Leuctra and Mantinea" (*). Noble and proud words and worthy of a hero! Nev-

---

(*) Epaminondas, Theban general who defeated the Spartans at Leuctra in 371 B. C. and was victorious and mortally wounded at Mantinea in 362 B. C.

ertheless there are other words more beautiful. *"Da mihi nesciri!"* (Grant me, O Lord,
to remain unknown!) Thus spoke the author
of the most beautiful book ever penned by the
hand of man—we do not here consider the
inspired Gospel—and this wish of the sublime
author of the Imitation has been realized for
five centuries: he has remained hidden behind
his masterpiece, greater in his effacement
than the Thebean in the exaltation of his
name. (*) One should not despise the love of
glory when it becomes a stimulant to great actions, but we must admit that Christian humility has been productive of greater actions
and of actions which cost less to society. To
reverse the role of these two motives and to
exalt the former at the expense of the latter
would be a step backward in civilization.

It would have been less objectionable if, in
reviving the passion of antiquity for the per-
petuation of one's name, the humanists of the
Renaissance had at least followed the noble
idea of Epaminondas and not the manner of
the pedants. For most of them were pedants
indeed, dreaming that immortality might
come to them from a well-turned distich, or
a new expression, or a pleasant saying. Read

(*) "The Imitation of Christ" was at first published
anonymously in A. D. 1418. Its authorship was until recently in dispute, being attributed to various spiritual writers, St. Bernard, St. Bonaventure, Innocence III, Walter Hilton,
Giovanni Gersen and others. The authorship of Thomas
a Kempis has been completely established in recent years.

in the *Femmes Savantes* of Molière the scene
between Trissotin and Vadius, and you will
have acquaintance with almost all the pagan
and semi-pagan humanists of the Renaissance.
In their books, in their correspondence, in their
conversation, there is in evidence a childish
vanity, an extreme susceptibility, an amazing
infatuation. If you but seem to touch with
disrespectful hands one of the rays of their
halo, at once these demi-gods will turn against
you in coarse invectives, hurl at your head all
the abuse of the fishwoman's vocabulary, forgetting that, though immortals, they are talking and acting as street porters! This is all
the more pitiful when one considers that,
with all their pretensions to renown, most of
these great men have drawn on posterity letters of exchange which posterity has allowed
to be protested. Erasmus of Rotterdam, our
quasi-compatriot, is the most celebrated and
the most estimable type of this class of minds.
In his own time he was adulated as a god and
actually looked upon himself as a guiding
genius, whilst he was simply a bookman
crammed with Latin and Greek, although we
must admit that he had well digested these
languages.

If from the thinkers we pass on to the men
of action, we shall find paganism put into
practice with astounding boldness. At this
time we find a legion of men who had entirely
given up the Christian idea that they might

conform to the pagan morality of pleasure and success. They abounded in all ranks of society, were not lacking among the clergy, and, alas, were to be found even on the Chair of Peter. Pope Alexander VI is the most sinister incarnation of paganism under the tiara: serene and smiling amidst the mire of vices, he displayed with an astonishing lack of conscience the spectacle of his turpitudes; and even in the winter of old age, he prolonged, beneath the eyes of an astonished world, the wild revel of an existence lacking in moral sense.

Alexander VI is the type of the voluptuary —nothing more. (*) His son Caesar Borgia presents to us the most finished type of the pagan politician. Young, beautiful, brave, intelligent, friend of the arts, model of courtesy, he is, in spite of all these external qualities, the most cruel, the most perverse, the most unscrupulous of men. The conquest of the greatest possible power and glory is for him the only ideal of life, and it seems never

---

* Inasmuch as an authority like Kurth, and the best Catholic historians generally, have agreed in a very unfavorable judgement of Alexander VI, it is very interesting to note that the Rt. Rev. P. De Roo, author of the "History of America before Columbus" maintains that the verdict of history regarding Alexander VI should be entirely reversed, that the case of this Pontiff is an astonishing case of complete calumniation by the hostile writers of his time. Monsignor De Roo has published "Materials for a History of Pope Alexander VI, his Relatives and his Times" in five volumes, in which he supports his contention by means of hitherto unstudied documents, especially from the secret archives of the Vatican. In the first volume he contends that Caesar Borgia was not the son of Alexander VI, but the son of Alexander's first nephew. The Encyclopedia Press, New York, 1924.

to have entered his mind that such an ideal
could be limited by any moral law. "There
is nothing in common between religion and
politics! Politics is an art which one culti-
vates for itself and which knows but one law,
that of success." Thus Caesar Borgia was
taught by his master, the most genial, the
most atrocious of all the representatives of
the Renaissance, the man whose name has
been given to a political system of deceit and
immorality, a system which utterly ignores
Christianity:—this man is Nicholas Machiavelli.

Strikingly expressive is the portrait of
this heartless and unfeeling genius, which
may be seen today in the Uffizi Gallery at
Florence. Note the excessively sharp pro-
file, the cruel fox-like snout, where you may
read the combination of sanguinary baseness
of instinct and wonderful acumen of mind:
you will catch yourself shivering, and you
will quickly turn away with an impression
of uneasiness and fright. Moreover Machiavelli has left us a portrait of himself in his
writings, especially in his treatise *The Prince*
which for centuries has been the breviary of
absolute monarchs, even of those who wrote
anti-Machiavellian books, as Frederick II of
Prussia (*). It is not necessary to state that

---

* Charles V was a reader of Machiavelli. His ungallant
remark at the raising of the siege of Metz: **Fortune is a woman, she does not love old men,** was inspired by **"The Prince"**
of Machiavelli, ch. XXV.—G. K.

Machiavelli had no more morals than faith, and that this almost diabolical contemner of the Papacy led a private life which was but a tissue of infamies.

I have mentioned only a few characteristic types; but in order to make known all the varieties of pagan celebrities of this epoch, it would be necessary to give other names— beginning with Lorenzo della Valle,who boldly professed in his writings the principles of the most abject epicurism, down to Pomponazzi, who did not fear to deny the doctrine of the immortality of the soul and who ended his life by suicide. To give an idea of the moral and intellectual atmosphere of the time, one should at least recall the extraordinary for- tune of the ignoble Aretino, a sort of Leo Taxil of the sixteenth century, though possessing more talent, before whom princes trembled, and who touched the pocket-books of kings who feared the power of this pamphleteer. All these persons, by their talent, by their boldness, by their number, and through skilful grouping, give the impression that they are the true representatives of their time, the general expression of the spirit of the Renaissance. And, indeed, if the intellectual movement which bears this name must be judged by the men who took control of it, it is certain that the Renaissance was à return to the ideas and the aspirations of paganism. We deny

this conclusion because we reject the premises
—but it was very easy to be deceived therein.

Some condemned whole movement because of its abuses.

People were deceived from the first. Many
sincere minds were alarmed at the unheard of
licentiousness of thought, often followed by
a like licentiousness of morals, and they attributed to the intellectual movement itself
the scandals which were but an abuse.
They decried art, literature and science,
because they held these to be directly responsible for the moral and religious crisis of
their time. Seeing that intellectual culture
produced such fruits, they turned from it
and confined themselves to divine science.
This is, alas, to-day as then, the conduct
of honest people who have more good
will than keenness of mind, in whom are
verified the words of the Gospel that the
children of darkness are wiser in their
generation than the children of light. The
temptation to act thus is so strong that,
for the greater number, it is well-nigh irresistible. It is so expeditious, so convenient, for
minds of narrow vision, to condemn as a whole
all intellectual and social progress because of
the abuses to which it gives occasion!

This narrowness of view, though it usually
shelters itself under the cloak of religion,
really injures religion by making it appear
opposed to all progress and incompatible with

every development of civilization. This is
not the broad and vivifying spirit of Christianity, it is the narrow-mindedness of the
grossest fanaticism which dictates, at all
epochs, the attitude of reactionaries. "If
these books say the same things as the Koran,
they are useless; if they say the contrary,
they are hurtful; in either case, they must be
burned." This language is worthy of Calif
Omar setting fire to the library of Alexandria; but it is too often held by zealous Christians, without suspecting that they are such
good Mussulmans! It was, for instance, in
1507, the language of Adrian de Corneto, who
using other words of comparison, strove to
establish that all science is contained in Holy
Writ and that it is folly to seek it elsewhere.

It was likewise the language of the rigorists
of the moral order, who correctly attributed the
corruption of their time to luxury, and who imagined that they could remedy it by bringing
back the people, if need be by force, to the
simplicity of morals and to the observance of
the evangelical counsels. They dreamed of
changing the world into a vast convent where
each inhabitant would be subject to the severe
observance of monastic rules, and where in
a gigantic auto-da-fe they would burn, to-day
all the products of frivolous and corrupt-
ing luxury, to-morrow all those who would
not foreswear its worship. What a beautiful
dream for high and visionary minds, who

thought they could do without human liberty
in the establishment of the Kingdom of God!
So they often dreamed in those republics
partly democratic, partly theocratic, such as
the Puritans founded in the American colo-
nies,and Calvin (*) in the Commune of Ge--
neva. We recognize the same character in the
enterprise of that high-minded enthusiast,
the monk Jerome Savonarola, whose noble
ideals and sincere zeal for the Catholic faith
are beyond question. This unfortunate reformer was dictator of Florence long enough
to get the notion that he had realized his ideal
and also to draw upon himself the furious
opposition which brought him to the funeral
pile.

Savonarola did not understand the law
of growth which rules mankind, as it rules
nature, and which does not permit society—
any more than the individual—to have the
same manners and the same mode of life in
its old age as in its early years. Like the individual, humanity passes through various
phases and while it always retains its
elemental character it presents a diversity
in its manifestations. Gradually, as it
advances, it strips itself of the traits of

(*) Calvin, John, born at Noyon, France, 1509, and
died at Geneva, 1564. In Geneva the clergy, assisted by the
elders, governed despotically and in detail the actions of
every citizen. In this matter Geneva set an example to the
later Puritans, who did all in their power to imitate its
discipline.

youth to put on those of old age; it loses
buoyancy to gain experience; it gathers the
fruits of its former labors, extends its knowledge, sweetens the relations among men,
studies itself and calls to its activities the control of the moralist and of the scientist. In
thus developing itself according to its nature,
society does not put itself in contradiction
to Christianity, because the faith of Jesus
Christ does not condemn any human faculty
nor demand of civilization the sacrifice of any
of its conquests, provided these labors and all
the enjoyments which flow from them remain
subordinate to the higher law of charity.
When then, righteously moved by the miser-
ies of his time, Savonarola thought to remedy
them by reforms which offended nature and
which were worse than the evil itself, he acted
blindly and was bound to provoke the frightful reaction of which he himself was the first
and most pathetic victim.

The Catholic Church on the contrary headed the movement in the right direction.

The Catholic Church did not enter the way
into which Savonarola wished to draw her.
In face of the great movement of the Renaissance, she remembered her eternal mission;
she recalled not only that she is the religion
of people still in infancy and of poor communities, but also that she is to lead to God
the rich nations and enlightened civilization.

Far from cursing the riches of science and the opulence of arts—though she often saw them misused—she blessed them and wished to make them contribute to the glory of God and the salvation of souls. And, with this largeness of view and this boldness of enterprise which we have recognized in her in former crises, instead of opposing the future and being crushed by it, instead of holding aloof and being left behind, she boldly grasped the banner of intellectual progress and headed the movement which drew humanity towards its mighty destinies.

I do not say that this attitude of the Church towards the Renaissance was always the result of formal deliberation, or that the chiefs of the hierarchy were always conscious of the fateful bearing of the part they played. Were they themselves, as private persons, not subject to the charm of artistic and literary life; and does not their surrender to the seductions that surrounded them sufficiently explain the interest of the Church in art and literature? And were there not among them some who became intoxicated with the wine of the Renaissance to the point of totally forgetting the Catholic spirit, forgetting that they were priests, bishops, cardinals, remembering only that they were humanists? But it is precisely because the movement was of such intensity that one is astonished that, instead of allowing herself to be drawn on by the current, the Church should have undertaken to direct it and that she should have succeeded in a large measure. She did not cry anathema against it, as the busy-bodies would have wished; she did not sacrifice the legitimate demands of the Christian spirit, as did the Humanists; she proposed to create, in the full meaning of the term, a revival which would be Catholic—and she succeeded. The names of Pius II, Nicholas V, Julius II, and Leo X recall the most powerful and the most efficacious protection which the intellectual life of the human race ever received from a sovereign authority.

I do not intend here to recount in detail the history of this incomparable patronage of science, art, and literature, or to show the Sovereign Pontiffs surrounded by the glorious phalanx of artists—at their head the unrivaled Bramante (1), Michelangelo (2) and

---

(1) Bramante (1444-1514) Italian painter and architect designed St. Peter's in Rome. His work in Milan is characterized by a pronounced picturesque decorative style, whilst his artistic productions in Rome are, as far as possible, free from all external decorations, and impressive by reason of their proportions, grandeur, and power.

(2) Michelangelo (Buonarotti), 1475-1564, Italian sculptor, painter, and arctitect, one of the greatest artists of all times. At the request of Pope Julius II he painted the world-renowned frescoes of the Creation, the Fall, the Preparation for the coming of the Redeemer, and the Last Judgment, in the Sistine Chapel of the Vatican.

the divine Raphael (*). But I may say in general and without fear of exaggeration that no century has seen—that probably no century will ever see — such an ensemble of works as the Dome of St. Peter's, the Sistine Chapel, the Stanze and the Loggie of the Vatican. If — unlike Jerusalem, Antioch, Athens, Bagdad, and Cordova—Rome is not today a tomb in ruins, with her grandeur forever destroyed; if the Eternal City is ever resplendent, in the eyes of the entire world, with the incomparable splendor which surrounds her sanctuaries, her museums, her libraries; if the world does not cease to go to her in pilgrimage as to the living center of civilization, it is to the Popes of the Renaissance that she is indebted. It is not the ruins of some monuments of antiquity which would entitle her, in the eyes of the world, so far to outrank Athens with its Parthenon, or Treves with its *Porta Nigra*. The Popes have made the Eternal City a page of apologetics, written under their dictation by the greatest artists of the world, a page which will speak from century to century with superhuman eloquence.

But here, as in all other things, Rome is but the symbol of the Catholic Church herself.

(*) Raphael (Raffaele Sanzio d'Urbino), 1483-1520 Italian painter, the founder of the Roman school of painting of the Renaissance, preeminent as a draftsman, a colorist, and a master of graceful composition and remarkable for the wide range of his subjects and the great variety of his style. He painted the world-famed "Transfiguration" and "Sistine Madonna."

Thanks to the Popes of the Renaissance, the
Catholic Church wears henceforth upon her
brow a new tiara, which renders her sacred
even in the eyes of those who despise the
Renaissance: it is the threefold crown of
science, of art, and of poetry. She has taken
under her patronage these three, the
proudest and the freest in the world, and
accompanied by them, she marches on through
history in dazzling glory and magnificence.
In accordance with the wish of the dying
Nicholas V, set forth in a discourse which
seems to express the mind of this great Pope
and his life better than any other document,
she subjugates the human imagination and
compels admiration by the incomparable
prestige of her esthetic greatness.

One feels this deeply when at Rome, under
the lofty cupola which shelters the tomb of
the Fisherman of men and from which shines
forth in gigantic letters this divine sentence: "Thou art Peter, and upon this
rock I will build my Church." No one, I
think, can wholly escape the spell of these
surroundings: neither the Christian who feels
his heart expand, nor the indifferent one who
finds again a remnant of Catholic joy and
pride, nor the dissenter who must feel in his
inmost heart a melancholy regret for the
broken unity of the ancient Christian faith.
As to the enemies of the Church, however intense their hatred, however vicious the blows

they deal her, they feel here more than elsewhere the presence of Him Who has said:
"The wicked shall see, and shall be angry, he
shall gnash with his teeth and pine away; the
desire of the wicked shall perish." (Ps.
III., 11).

Importance of stand taken by Church at this turning
point of history.

This is, I think, the aspect under which we
must consider the role of the Church and of
the Papacy at this turning point of history,
known as the Renaissance. I am aware that
this is not the opinion of everyone. There are
to-day many people, especially among the best
Christians and among those who aim to restore Catholic inspiration to art and poetry,
who regret the great part taken by the Church
in the work of the Renaissance. They think
that she protected the Humanists and the artists more than she should have done, that she
did not safeguard the tradition of Catholic
art and Catholic thought against the new
ideas, and that she needlessly sacrificed to
the taste of the time the elements of Christian
vitality. They would almost picture paganism invading the sanctuaries and making the
Church of Christ the prisoner of the age.

And certainly, as I have hinted above, there
is no lack of circumstances to give to this
judgment an appearance of truth. By bringing together all the data furnished by the
shocking chronicles of the sixteenth century,

in Rome as elsewhere, by gathering such say-
ings and such actions of princes of the
Church as were manifestly opposed to the law
of God, it would be easy to paint a picture
which would call forth strong condemnation.
But likewise, one might take the opposite elements and picture a society worthy of the
first centuries of Christianity. But history
need not resort to special pleading.

The truth is that if the Church, in face
of the widespread intellectual movement
whose origin and character we have considered, had confined herself to protest and reaction and had wrapped herself in tradition
as does the vanquished soldier in the folds of
his flag, she would have permitted civilization to leave her behind; she would have lost all
contact with the future and would have had
no influence upon the elite of mankind; she
would have become a closed chapel where the
faithful—dwindling in numbers day by day—
would meet only to weep over ruins and to
anathematize the age. We should be thankful
that she resisted the temptation and that,
thanks to the wisdom of the Popes, she rose
to the height of the movement of the sixteenth
century, that she has remained abreast of the
times down to the twentieth century, and that
she will not fail to keep pace with all the
movements of future ages. The essential
point is that, in throwing open her sanctuaries to the new intellectual life of mankind,

she did not sacrifice a particle of the higher
truth, a single commandment of the moral
law, a single article of her creed. No doubt,
it was difficult at times to reconcile the
severe requirements of the eternal laws with
the bold movements of the modern spirit, and
often the moralist and the lover of the beautiful must have been shocked at the poorly
veiled contradictions which resulted from the
union of the Church and the Renaissance.
But it is none the less true that the Church
of the sixteenth century has handed down intact the patrimony of primitive Christianity.

An anecdote which I read for the first time
in the beautiful History of the Popes by Pastor presents this thought in so expressive a
manner that I cannot resist the pleasure of
repeating it as the crowning point of this
lecture.

Julius II, as you all know, had asked Bramante, the greatest and boldest genius of the
Renaissance, to re-build the Basilica of St.
Peter on the Vatican Hill. Bramante combined boundless faith in the principles of
his art with contempt of the past—a failing
common to nearly all the artists of that epoch.
He began by demolishing the ancient Vatican
Basilica which, it is true, threatened to col-
lapse, but he acted with a haste and lack of
respect that were inexcusable. In the boldness of his genius, he went even further. In
order to make the new church more imposing,

he wished to change its orientation and, for his purpose, he thought of moving the tomb which, for fifteen centuries, has been the inviolate asylum of the sacred remains of the Prince of the Apostles. But on this point Pope Julius II, who so far had granted every request of his artist, gave a categorical refusal. Bramante would not be silenced; he brought forward a number of reasons, some from considerations of art, others from the view-point of religion. He contended that if the tomb were moved as he desired it would be in better harmony with the enlarged edifice and would add to the piety of the faithful; in a word, he used every argument and pleaded with a vehemence and an obstinacy which seemed likely to triumph in the end. But the Pope was inexorable; he declared that under no consideration would he allow any one to touch the tomb of him upon whom Jesus Christ had built the universal Church. Art had to give way to religion. The remains of St. Peter were not taken from their crypt and the orientation of the church was not changed.

This story is significant. It tells friends and enemies alike that the Catholic Church accommodates herself to all progress of thought and to all forms of art, but that—built upon the rock of the eternal truths—she permits no one to change the axis of the world which she has set towards Heaven.

The Church and the Revolution

On May 5, 1789, there convened at Versailles the States-General of France (*). Surely no one could have then foretold that within less than five years royalty would be suppressed, that the king and queen would be put to death, that the dauphin would die a slow death in a cobbler's shop, that the nobility would have to choose between the guillotine and exile, that the Catholic religion would be proscribed, that a girl of the demi-monde would ascend the altar of Notre Dame of Paris under the name of Goddess of Reason and that, among the deputies who took part in the procession, there would be one, the most ridiculous, the most awkward, and perhaps the most shallow of them all, who would cut the throats of most of his colleagues. Had such a prediction been made, it would have met with derision and indignation. This series of unlikely suppositions, dramatized after their occurrence by La Harpe, in his famous *Prédication*

(*) In order to reform existing abuses Louis XVI, in compliance with the universal request of all classes of the French people, convened the States-General, or the assembly of the three orders of th kingdom, namely, the Clergy, the Nobility, and the Third Estate or Commonality. These had not been in session since 1614.

de Cazotte, falls far short of the frightful realities which sank the ancient regime into an
abyss of blood.

Revolution unforeseen.

There had been nothing to foretell the awful catastrophe to the generation which witnessed those scenes unprecedented in the annals of history. Apart from certain black
specks which could forebode no evil except to
the most trained eye, the sky was serene and
the morrow seemed favorable. The dynasty
was popular; this had been very evident at the
birth of the dauphin. The election records of
1789 attest that the immense majority of vot-
ers were sincerely devoted to religion and to
royalty alike. It is true that various reforms
were demanded; but all these, or almost all,
had to do with undeniable abuses, which were
no longer defended by any one, not even by
those who profited by them. And then the
gentleness of manners was such that there
was nothing to fear even from the most energetic reformers. Every one boasted of being
a sensible man, just as in other times, one
would have been ashamed of it. Literature,
that supreme authority of the epoch, took
more and more the character of the idyl. An
atmosphere of benevolence seemed about to
envelop and permeate all society. People had
acquired such reliance in the native goodness
of humanity and in the excellence of the prin-

ciples of philosophy that they loved to think
of the future under the aspect of a golden age,
which they believed they were about to attain.
The first measures of the Constituent Assembly (1), voted by acclamation and often on
the motion of the privileged classes themselves,
were not such as to open the eyes of men.
The Feast of the Federation (July 14, 1790)
was, in this respect, a real illusion. Every one
believed that the pact of human fraternity
had been sealed on the basis of liberty. The
error was of long duration. They were still
exchanging love kisses long after claps of
thunder had been heard in the peaceful sky.
Even the imagination of the sinister cut-
throats held fast to the vision of the great human pastoral. It was in an azure-colored gar-
ment, with a sheaf of ears of grain and flowers in hand, that the sensible Robespierre (2),
the eloquent opponent of capital punishment,
was to celebrate the feast of the Supreme Be-

---

(1) The Third Estate, having as many members as the
other two orders of the States-General combined, insisted on
voting per head instead of per order, and thus obtained the
preponderance in the States-General. The new assembly thus
formed with the Third Estate in control was called the Constituent Assembly, because it had for its object the forma-
tion of a constitution.

(2) Robespierre, born at Arras, May 6, 1759. He was
a lawyer; was elected to the Third Estate of the States-
General in 1789; became the leader of the Extreme Left in
the Constituent Assembly, and one of the foremost orators of
the Revolution. He was elected deputy to the Convention in
1792; was identified with the "Reign of Terror"; was overthrown in the Convention July 27, 1794, the 9th Thermidor,
year II of the Republican calendar, and guillotined the next
day.

ing on an altar in mid-air. He dreamed, no doubt, of the welfare of the human race, of the sweetness of country life, of the charms of virtue and innocence—and this but a few days before the frightful awakening of the ninth of Thermidor!

Purpose of Revolution destruction of ancient regime.

If conditions were such, how explain this atrocious Revolution, this hideous debauch, whither sacrilegious folly and sanguinary impiety led dismayed humanity for years? How understand this vertigo which, at a given moment, took hold of the first nation of the world, and made it turn round and round and stagger like a drunken man, and so affected it that up to the present it has not recovered its former stability? Are these the necessary crises which accompany the bringing forth of a new world? Are they the agonizing convulsions of an ancient civilization? Are they the tragical phases of that gigantic struggle between two powers which is going on forever for the possession of society—the struggle between good and evil, between truth and error, between God and Satan?

Certainly it would be idle to attribute the Revolution to the abuses of the ancient regime. It would be assigning a most insignificant cause to an effect whose proportions are almost beyond calculation. There have been abuses at all times, and when the

French Revolution burst forth there were
abuses elsewhere as well as in France. But
there was not everywhere else, as in France, a
most sincere good will, on the part of the ruling classes, to extirpate abuses. Louis XVI,
who was called *the best of kings,* set the example in this respect. He restored to the
Protestants their civil rights, he suppressed
the rack, he convened the Assembly of
the Notables (*), and when, finally, he
took the initiative in calling together
the States-General (which had not been
in session since 1614) it was to bring
about the collaboration of the king and
his people in working out the necessary
reforms. There was the same good will,
the same sincerity among the two privileged
classes, namely the clergy and the nobility.
They both generously sacrificed their most
precious prerogatives for the sake of public
peace and the general welfare, the clergy with
spontaneous resignation, the nobility with
rather thoughtless enthusiasm. Never before
had privileged classes renounced their privileges for reasons of patriotism and philosophy. It may be said that if the Revolution
had risen to do away with abuses, it would

(*) The Assembly of Notables, a council of prominent
persons from the three classes of the State convoked by the
kings on extraordinary occasions. The most famous assemblies were those of 1787 and 1788, summoned by Louis XVI.
In the assembly of 1787 there were only twenty-seven representatives of the Third Estate out of a total of a hundred
and forty-four members.

have come to a close after the night of the
Fourth of August, 1789, that is, when it had
hardly begun.

It is therefore false to pretend that the
Revolution was caused by the abuses of the
ancient regime. The Revolution was more
than a mere effort to resist abuses which
had ceased to exist before it triumphed. Its
purpose—if it had a purpose at all—was not
the reform of the regime, but its destruction.
A blind, irresistible force, it acted with all
the power of a furious element let loose and
it overthrew society from top to bottom, up-
rooting everything after the manner of a
cyclone, leaving the ground strewn with ruins
wherever it had passed. But, as in meteor-
ology one may give reasons for the appearance of cyclones, so also, in history, the outburst of similar catastrophes may be traced
to its causes.

Free thought one of the causes of Revolution.

The revolutionary spirit is far anterior to
the Revolution. In France, as elsewhere, one
may trace it back to the Renaissance from
which it proceeds as the river flows from the
glacier. The Renaissance, as we have seen,
had developed two parallel currents whose
junction, at a given moment, had become the
great destructive force. The first current,
that of free thought, held course among the
cultured classes; the other, that of free en-

joyment, had its source in high society. For a long time, the freethinkers held aloof, with a disdainful indifference for the great religious struggles. They saw in these nothing but the quarrels of bigots, and when they became involved in them, it was to strike with the weapon of irony the one of the two combatants who at the time appeared the more formidable. Christianity under all its forms inspired them with equal aversion. Their admiration went out only to pagan antiquity, which had neither dogmas to bridle the mind nor priesthood to interpret its dogmas. Encamped on the field of pure naturalism, they waited the moment when Protestantism, which unconsciously had prepared the way for them, would have finished beating down the buttresses of the temple, that they might then hurl themselves against the noble edifice with sap and hammer.

Being revolutionaries of a special kind, they did not oppose the civil power to any great extent, first because they saw in royal absolutism a fair realization of their ideal of pagan politics, also because they were not eager for martyrdom. The spirit of free thought did not yield to the movement of the Catholic Restoration which marked so brilliantly the opening annals of the seventeenth century; but flowed beneath as an undercurrent and finally reappeared to be denounced by the thundering voice of Bossuet (*), at the threshold of the eighteenth century. Then it emptied its filthy waters upon a world prepared to receive it. It then made up for its long enforced silence. From Fontenelle, who said that he would not open his hand even were it full of truth, to Bayle who opened wide a hand filled with sophisms and lies, the distance is not perceptible from the viewpoint of chronology but, for him who looks beneath the surface, what a road was travelled between *l'Histoire des Oracles,* published by Fontenelle in 1687, and the *Dictionnaire Philosophique* by Bayle, which appeared in 1697! In the former we have still the elegant scepticism of the man of the world, who slips a discreet doubt in a happy phrase, in a good word, in a smile; in the latter we have open and cynical unbelief in all its brutality. As has been aptly remarked, all Voltaire is found in the *Dictionnaire Historique.* The role of the patriarch of Ferney consisted in popularizing the philosophy of Bayle and in giving it a militant and aggressive character.

(*) Bossuet, Jacques-Bénigne, a celebrated French writer and pulpit orator (1627-1704), was appointed preceptor to the Dauphin for whose benefit he wrote, among other things, the greatest book of the Century of Louis XIV: "Discourse on Universal History." Later he was appointed Bishop of Meaux. He is the author of numerous spiritual, historical polemical works, and, in the words of St. Simon, "died fighting." Ferdinand Brunetière, the eminent French critic, says: "There is nothing, in French, which surpasses a fine page of Bossuet."

Licentiousness another cause of Revolution.

Along with unbelief there grew up licentiousness of morals. Bred in high society, where man no longer saw anything in life but a round of pleasure, moral laxity had contaminated the entire court of Valois, and we find shameful traces of it in the well-known physiognomy of the Béarnais. Think of the morals of that society of which Brantome in the XVI century and Hamilton in the XVII century were the complaisant chroniclers! One is shocked at the cynicism and the frivolity with which men and women rushed headlong in the pursuit of the most unavowable pleasures. So long as Louis XIV lived, the prestige he gave to his reign concealed all these turpitudes under the broad folds of the royal purple, and men showed some decency, some respect of self and of others, even amid the most revolting excesses; but his death gave the signal for an unprecedented loosening of all moral restraint. I should offend my hearers, were I to indicate, even in the most discreet manner, the example set by the Regent and by Louis XV; but it must be said that it was followed very generally and that, with a few honorable exceptions, high society seemed anxious to make all France the home of wickedness. Never had Christian civilization witnessed so shameful a spectacle.

Unbelief and licentiousness fostered by Voltaire.

The two currents above mentioned had more than once mixed their muddy waters during the long years which preceded the advent of Voltaire; with him they became finally but the one current which was about to flood France. It was at the Hotel of the Temple, among the leaders of vice and impiety who then held their headquarters there, that the sinister pontiff of modern irreligion grew up. This friend of the *libertines* of high society was also on good terms with the notorious Ninon de Lenclos, who bequeathed to him two thousand francs for the purchase of books. It affords some satisfaction to know that the greatest enemy of the Christian faith should have been the protégé of a courtesan. For my part, when I consider that the "philosophy" comes to us from the boudoir of Ninon, I feel as did Tertullian who congratulated himself on the fact that the first persecutor of Christianity was Nero.

Voltaire was the most complete incarnation of the irreligious spirit of the eighteenth century. To the French corruption and frivolity he added the hateful fanaticism which he imbibed, while in England, from the deists of that country. After his return he was perhaps the most marvelous workman of destruction who has ever appeared. He was endowed with a mind unequalled in suppleness and vivacity, universally gifted as a writer, skilled in the infernal art of handling the poisonous weapon of sarcasm and irony; and, in the war to death which he had declared against Christianity, he employed all the resources of a mind exceptionally constituted for intellectual struggles and all the indefatigable activities of a satanic hatred against the Church. For almost a century, he led the irreligious campaign with astounding obstinacy and—to use the expression of a great modern poet—he was the missionary of the devil among the men of his time. He is little read nowadays, because, notwithstanding his prodigious talent, his works were of his day; nevertheless his mind remains the evil genius of the modern world, and, to the present day, the Christian cannot look upon his hideous likeness without feelings of fright and horror.

Gathered about Voltaire were all the defenders of impiety, or "philosophy," as they were pleased then to designate it. From this crowd came forth the *Encyclopedie,* a formidable engine of war which, under the pretext of presenting to the public a summary of modern knowledge, carried to all classes hatred and contempt of Christianity. *Ecrasez l'infâme!* (Crush the infamous thing!) was the watchword of the master; the disciples often outstripped their master. They found him bigoted, for they were atheists, while Voltaire honored God by believing in Him.

Banded together as organized leaders of public opinion, surrounded by the prestige of science, and winning fresh popularity from the mild opposition of the civil power, the Encyclopedists were able to undermine with impunity all religious belief, all the foundations of moral and social life. They succeeded, morover, in enlisting the co-operation of the civil power in their work. Revolutionaries in religious matters, they were, at least apparently, conservatives in politics. *Bold against God alone,* they knew how to spare the despots, how to glorify them when necessary. Were not the kings who hated religion the best of kings? This is why Voltaire cringed before Frederick II (1), before Catherine II (2), even before Madame de Pompadour, the notorious mistress of King Louis XV, indifferent as he was to everything save his combat against the faith of Jesus Christ. Provided he were given control of religion, nothing else concerned him, as he realized, no doubt, that this was all he needed. It would appear that at times, in the midst of his work of death, he caught a glimpse of what was to

---

(1) Frederick II, "The Great," King of Prussia, which country he raised to the rank of a great power. (1740-1788). He early became a free-thinker. He praised the literature of France and despised that of Germany. He was an intimate friend of Voltaire.

(2) Catherine II (1729-1796), empress of Russia, extended the limits of the Russian empire by victories over the Turks, secularized the property of the clergy, became famous as a writer, and corresponded with the French (Encyclopedists.

happen: "After me, they will see a fine racket," he wrote. This, however, was but a flash, and he went back at once to his accursed work.

Seductive theories of Rousseau impelling factor.

But if Voltaire did not draw political conclusions because he was too much in love with his own ease and because, in the main, he was still imbued with the ancient regime, there was one who was willing to draw these conclusions for him. This one, unlike the great lord who wished to die quietly in his beautiful solitude at Ferney, was a soured plebeian, ill-bred, suspicious, a misanthrope to a degree. Possessing the soul of a poet and the heart of a footman, Jean Jacques Rousseau hated and despised the society in which he lived, the civilization which surrounded him, all society and all civilization. He had all that was needed to make his revolutionary passions penetrate into the hearts of others: captivating warmth of expression, genuine sensibility, sincere emotion, enthusiasm for the good and the beautiful, or for what he believed to be such. He introduced a new strain into French literature. To the artificial society of the salons, he, the savage who had slept under the open sky, revealed the charms of nature; he gave a taste for the beauties of the landscape to the great lords who had never seen one except through the windows of their castles; at his voice, the entire court rose to go with Queen Marie Antoinette to contemplate the early dawn. Even Voltaire had his hour of infatuation!

Nevertheless, these are not the real triumphs of Jean Jacques. He had made far different discoveries in his musings as a lone walker. He had discovered that man is good when he comes from the hand of nature but becomes corrupted when he lives in the state of society. This is a heresy with an added sophism, because it denies original sin, and what is society but man? He had discovered that all the arts of civilization, and particularly science and literature, serve but to increase corruption. He had discovered that society is the result of a contract between its members and that the source of law is their will, which may express itself whenever it pleases. Away with religion, with morality, with tradition! The people are the only sovereign, and any institution, any law, any will opposed to the people is tyranny, usurpation, and high treason.

These were the political theories of Rousseau (*)which his eloquence and enthusiasm succeeded in fastening upon the minds of his contemporaries. A society which had been taught to scoff at the religious law and to be-

---

(*) Rousseau Jean Jacques born at Geneva, June 28, 1712; died near Paris, July 2, 1778. His book, "Contrat Social," has been styled "the Koran of the Revolutionists."

lieve in nothing was to accept with enthusiasm such seductive theories: accordingly the
doctrine of the *Contrat Social* became in a
short time the doctrine of the cultured public.
The disciples of Rousseau were legion, chiefly
among the classes whom the sarcasms of
Voltaire had turned away from religion and
who, having ceased to believe in the Christian
ideal, could not do without some kind of ideal
and thought they had found it in the dream-
ings of the sophist of Geneva.

But is it really true that the alliance between free thought and voluptuousness is sufficient to bring forth the revolutionary spirit?
Is it not true that elsewhere—as in England—
the ruling classes had displayed, with no less
cynicism than in France, their contempt for
the Christian faith and the moral law? Still
England did not cease to be the most conserv-
ative nation in the world. This is true, and it
would be interesting to follow closely the
energetic reaction whereby the English
people rid themselves of their own philosophers in order to come back to Christian tradition. But, without taking into account the
fact that the evil was more deeply rooted in
France, one must not forget that France is
the land where all ideas tend to be at once
translated into facts: in France less than elsewhere do people tolerate the contradiction
between the ideal and the reality. And the
French cultured classes had their ideal of po-

litical society, which had been elaborated by the Renaissance and perfected by the philosophy of the eighteenth century. This ideal, borrowed from ancient literature and adapted to modern society, was a dream of the imagination, an abstract conception evolved from pure reason; nothing seemed more urgent or more easy than the realization of this ideal. All that seemed necessary was to put it into effect by law and thus bring down to earth liberty, civic virtue, reason, philosophy and universal felicity.

Thus they thought. They were far removed from that faith in religion and in country which had caused Jean Racine (*) to write that truly Gallican sentence: "God has given me the grace never to be ashamed either of my king or of the Gospel." On the contrary, they were convinced that religion and monarchy or, as they expressed it, fanaticism and despotism caused all the evils of humanity. They thought that humanity, duped by priests and crushed by tyrants, would rise to the height of its glorious mission only when it would rid itself of priest and tyrant and give ear only to the teachings of philosophy. We have already spoken of the enthusiastic hope with which the sensible heart of the philosophers and their disciples looked for-

---

(*) Jean Racine, the most celebrated French tragic poet, born December 21, 1639; died at Paris, April 26, 1699. His master piece is "Athalie," a scriptural tragedy.

ward to the glad day. We must add that all
obstacles to the realization of their golden
dream, all reaction against the generous efforts they made for the public welfare en-
raged these gentle and humane mortals. They
considered every opposition a monstrous attempt against human liberty; and there
was no punishment which, in their anger,
they did not dream of inflicting on the criminal author. For their "philosophy" was a
religion; and if it did not send its heretics to
the funeral-pile, because of their horror of
the Inquisition, it found other means of
chastisement for contemners of its orthodoxy.
By way of anticipation, we may say that this
is all that the Revolution really discovered.

Philosophers put theories into practice—Revolution accomplished.

It is true that the philosophers and their
pupils were not the nation. But they were
its moving and active spirit, and, as is always
the case, it was easy to have others mistake
them for the nation. They were loud of
speech; though without authority, they spoke
in the name of the people and made themselves heard more and more every day; they
kept telling the people, as Sieyès expressed
it, that they had been nothing and that they
were to be everything. And scarcely had the
States-General reassembled when the philosophers took possession of the assembly in the

name of the nation, and pretended that the
other orders had no right and that the king
was merely their mandatory. Louis XVI had
imprudently taken the stand that the
States-General should vote by Orders,
whilst the Third Estate wished that they
should cast individual votes. At once it was
evident that the will of the Third Estate
placed itself above the will of the king. When
the master of ceremonies enjoined the Third
Estate to go to their own assembly hall and
leave that of the general meeting, President
Bailly replied: "I hold that the assembled
nation cannot be commanded." This saying,
more authentic than the one attributed to
Mirabeau, is also much more expressive: the
one, on the lips of the tribune, was the un-
authorized whim of a factionist; the other, in
the mouth of the President of the Third Estate, modest in its form but haughty in meaning, expressed the usurpation of all power by
the people.

The Revolution was accomplished. The
events which followed were but the logical development of this opening. And, if thirst
for blood and love of noise were not an integral part of the revolutionary spirit, then
it would be on June 23, 1789, and not on July
14, that the leaders of the France of today
should celebrate the anniversary of their
emancipation.

Thus was the ancient regime delivered

entirely into the hands of the States-General. They did with it as they pleased and left to the king only the doubtful privilege of endorsing their work, under the penalty of new riots. The "philosophers" were the masters of France. At last reason was to reign.

Poor showing of lawmakers.

But reason was to make a poor showing and the lawmakers were destined to fall far short of their task. As a whole, they formed a body singularly inexperienced and awkward, and at the same time presumptuous, in face of the gigantic task undertaken. Away from politics for centuries, the States-General did not know how to conduct associations of men. They were reformers in theory; they believed that the welfare of humanity could be enacted by laws, and they naïvely legislated patriotism and national happiness. As already stated, most of them were filled with classical recollections and impressed with the idea of the republican virtues which, in their student days, they had admired in the heroes of antiquity. They recalled these memories and enacted laws like college boys. Is there anything in the whole history of civilization more grotesque and at the same time more pitiable than the action of Hérault de Séchelles, President of the Convention, who, when they were about to draw up one of the many constitutions which the Revolutionaries gave to

France, sent to the National Library for the laws of Minos(*), in order to transcribe from them the laws he intended to give his country?

No wonder that the force of events, the laws of history, the laws of common sense should work havoc with the theses of Rousseau. Scarcely had the States-General informed the king that the people were the only sovereign, when there arose from the crowd a thousand threatening voices repeating to them what they had said to the king: "We are the sovereign people and you are but our mandatories!"

Revolutionary leaders overthrown.

And who spoke thus? Was it really the people of France? Not at all! The people were at their firesides, in the shops, behind the plow, engaged in fruitful and civilizing work; they had recorded their wishes in the election of 1789 and, whenever they were given an opportunity to express their will, they disavowed the intriguers and the malefactors who presumed to speak in their name. But what did these care? There being no longer any master in France—since on the fourteenth of July and the fifth of October, 1789, they had put aside the royal authority —they felt that they were the true masters of their country. They were organized, they

(*) Minos, ancient king of Crete, and lawgiver of that island.

knew what they wanted, they had under their thumb the king and the States-General against whom they could at pleasure incite well-planned riots; at one stroke they made June 20, August 10, May 31, the great revolutionary dates. It was in the clubs that they worked out the popular movements. In these clubs the most fanatical and the most unscrupulous were in control, and, in last analysis, two or three men—and these the worst of their kind—were the real sovereign people.

Taine, the well-known French critic and historian, in characterizing the triumvirate which controlled the destinies of France, has said that it was composed of a madman—Marat (1), of a savage—Danton (2), and of a pedant—Robespierre. These are the true sons of Voltaire and of Rousseau. Robespierre took the *Contrat Social* as his gospel; he had no other political education. With a handful of accomplices, these wretches went to work with no other aim, with no other ideal than to beat down all that stood in their way;

(1) Marat, born in Switzerland in 1744, assassinated at Paris in 1793, by Charlotte Corday. He was a leader of the Commune. He had two leading ideas which the committee of Public Safety subsequently realized—extermination in mass of the enemies of the Revolution and the appointment of a dictator, whose functions should be limited to proscribing.

(2) Danton, George-Jacques, born October 28, 1759; guillotined at Paris, April 5, 1794. He was an orator of great power, a leader of the attack of the Tuileries, was implicated in the "September massacres." He overthrew Hebert and his party with the aid of Robespierre and was in turn overthrown by the latter.

everything fell before them: first, the kings, nobles and priests, then all others who did not share their revolutionary ideal, all who were moderantist, as they put it in their jargon, the Feuillants (1), the Girondists (2), until having leveled all else—they set out to destroy one another. The Jacobins (3), cut the throats of the Cordeliers (4) the Thermidorians (5) cut the throats of the Jacobins, the Directory (6) deported the rest. Finally there came a dictator who, amid the plaudits of France, drove out the whole menagerie at the crack of the whip, and re-established for his own benefit the much despised despotism. The last revolu-

---

(1) Feuillants, a political faction of the Revolution which received its name from the convent of the Feuillants where it held its first meetings.

(2) Girondists, an important political party during the French Revolution. Their original leaders came from department of Gironde, hence their name. They were moderate Republicans, were the ruling party in 1792, were overthrown in the convention 1793.

(3) Jacobins, members of a society of French revolutionists organized in 1789, and called Jacobins from the Jacobin convent in Paris where they met. The more violent members speedily gained the control of the organization, supported Robespierre and brought on the "Reign of Terror."

(4) Cordeliers, a political club which took its name from its meeting place in the Convent of the Cordeliers. Its first political move was to demand the deposition of the king and the establishment of a republic, on June 20, 1791. It was extinguished with the "Reign of Terror" in 1794. Danton was its political chief.

(5) Thermidorians, the more moderate party of the French Revolution, who took part in or sympathized with the overthrow of Robespierre and his adherents on the 9th of Thermidor, year II. (July 27, 1794).

(6) The Directory, a body of five men who held the executive power in France from November 1, 1795, to the Coup d'état of 1799, November 9. The Directory was over-thrown by Napoleon, and succeeded by the Consulate.

tionaries became his footmen and his courtiers; he gave them golden liveries with which they were well pleased and one of them, having become a prince of the Empire, said to his old comrades of the Montagne (1): "In public, be sure to call me Your Excellency, but among ourselves call me simply Monseigneur." (2)

This is amusing, no doubt, and the enemies of the Revolution may find amusement at seeing the tragedy end in a farce. But what is more serious is the fact that, before making honorable amends in the ante-chambers of the new Caesar, the revolutionary spirit had time to invade all Europe and to spread everywhere the evil germ from which we suffer to the present day. The evil of the Revolution is the pretension to treat political society as if it were the creation of pure reason, independent of the action of the divine laws which rule the life of the world and of humanity!

This, in a few words, is the origin of the French Revolution. Long before its realization it was in the minds and the hearts of men; its success was brought about by the abdication or complicity of all the forces which should have opposed it. It was the

(1) Montagne (The Mountain). Name given to the extreme Revolutionary party in the legislatures of the first French Revolution. The name was derived from the fact that they occupied the higher part of the hall. Among the chief Montagnards were Robespierre and Danton.

(2) This anecdote is told of Cambacérès by Baron, Mosaïque Belge, 1837, p. 183.

breaking out of the malady at once intellectual and moral which for a long time had been working on the nation, coming down from the ruling classes to the rank and file of the citizens where it was transformed into a political catastrophe.

Revolution could have been avoided.

Could this catastrophe have been avoided? Unhesitatingly I answer yes, and I add that it would have been avoided if the Catholic Church had been there. But the Church was not there to help France. The Church, from the time of the XIV century, had been excluded from the political councils; it had been looked upon by the kings as a stranger—even as a rival; it had been enslaved to the point of having to sacrifice the Society of Jesus to the importunities of Freemasonry; (*) it

(*)   When Clement XIV ascended the throne of Peter, France, Spain and Portugal had suppressed the Society of Jesus de facto; the accession of a new Pope was made the occasion for insisting on the abolition of the Order, root and branch, de facto et de jure, in Europe and all over the world. This persecution was inspired in Latin countries by French irreligious philosophism, by Jansenism, Gallicanism and Erastianism. An ever-recurring and almost solitary grievance against the Society was the Fathers disturbed the peace wherever they were firmly established. The accusation was not unfounded; the Jesuits did, and to the present day do, disturb the peace of the enemies of the Church.

In 1772 the Spanish ambassador threatened the Pope with a schism in Spain and probably in other Latin countries, such as had existed in Portugal from 1760 to 1770. This contemptible threat broke the backbone of the opposition of Clement XIV who, the following June, signed the brief of suppression to restore the peace of the Church by removing one of the contending parties from the battlefield. No blame was laid by the Pope on the rules of the Order, or the personal conduct of the members, or the orthodoxy of their teaching.

had been deprived of its rights so that it was
no longer allowed to teach the doctrine of the
infallibility of the Sovereign Pontiff; it had
been watched and tracked even in its liturgy;
so that the Church in France was nothing
more than one of the wheels put in motion by
the despotism of the State.   The Gallican
Church had permitted the lay power to impose upon it the doctrine of the four articles,
which was a bold encroachment of the State
upon an exclusively doctrinal domain.   She
received at the hands of the king dogmas
which she rejected from the hand of the Pope.
It was of no benefit to her that she formed a
privileged   Order;   this   condition,   favorable on the surface, was an incessant source
of loss and unpopularity.   Associated, as she
was, with the destinies of the civil power,
she became conjointly liable and public opinion held her responsible for all the mistakes
of the regime of which she was a part.   She
was out of contact with the public spirit, had
at her disposal no lever to move the minds of
men, and was without influence in the world
of ideas.

It was unfortunate that all dignitaries of
the Church were chosen exclusively from the
nobility, at a time when the nobility had
fallen into general disfavor.   At one time—
the time of Louis XIV—there had been in the
ranks of the higher clergy some children of
the bourgeoisie who did not cut so bad a fig-

ure on episcopal thrones—one of these was
Bossuet. But when the revolution burst forth,
among the hundred and thirty bishops of the
kingdom of France, there was not one plebeian! Taken as a whole, the episcopate was
commendable in private life and was not
wanting in good qualities; but what a gulf
between it and the nation, what a source of
misunderstanding! The higher clergy—noble,
attached to the court, absentees, worldly, almost laicized—did not rise to the occasion;
they had neither the prestige of learning, nor
the eclat of great virtue, nor the advantage
of real popularity: they were not the kind to
guide the Church through the tempests.

Nor were the inferior clergy more abreast
of the times. True, they gave the example of
Christian virtue, and stood intact in a gan-
grened society. Tocqueville gives this magnificent testmonial: "I began the study of the
ancient society filled with prejudices against
it, I finished it filled with respect." Other
witnesses speak in the same manner and
everyone knows the heroism of the French
clergy in weathering the stormy days of the
Revolution. But, if they were well preserved
from a moral point of view, they no longer
had the true notion of the full part they were
to play in society. They languished in a general state of dejection, they were resigned to
be nothing, they did not protest when they
saw the Church humiliated. As a keen ob-

server has remarked *, they lacked *intellectual courage* and were, in a word, more ready for martyrdom than for the apostolate. And what is still worse, a great many of them, ignorant of the beauty of the social doctrine of Catholicism, allowed themselves to be won over by the doctrine of Rousseau; and they applauded, as if these were discoveries made by the philosophers, the few particles of truth which were really Catholic doctrine. To such an extent had the social and political traditions been obliterated even among the clergy! I know of nothing so painful as the illusion of those pastors who—the guardians of a treasure—allow counterfeit money to be substituted for the genuine coin!

Thus, the most heartrending spectacle of that whole century was not the deafening cries of error and crime but the silence of the Catholic Church concerning social truth. All lying doctrines were heard—but the Church of God was dumb. Her voice was the only one which did not rise in the din of discordant voices which characterizes the eighteenth century as noisy and strange. The century listened in vain for a teacher endowed with authority and eloquence to propound the luminous and sound teachings of the Catholic faith on the nature of society, on the mission

---

* L'abbé Sicard, Le clergé de l'ancien régime, les évêques, t. II, p. 114.

of the State and of the civic powers. These
lofty ideas were the only ones without defenders, but there was no sophism which did
not find as advocate some man of talent or of
genius.

Do we appreciate what would have happened if, during the ages which saw the
apogee of the monarchy, there had arisen
bishops, priests and laymen to proclaim the
eternal social principles of Christianity—who,
going beyond the Renaissance to the great
doctors of the Middle Ages, would have taught
an astonished world that there is such a thing
as Christian politics not to be confounded
with the politics of royal absolutism but which
contains at once the eternal truths and their
applications, *nova et vetera?* Do we realize
what would have happened if, like Fénelon in
his *Plan de Gouvernement* written for the
Duke of Burgundy, they had protested
against the enslavement of the Church, demanded for her *freedom as in Turkey* (*),
preached the suppression of the unbridled
luxury of the court, branded all abuses and
sought means to remedy the evils of society?
May we not believe that they would have been
heeded? Would not the destinies of the world
have been changed if, when the problem of so-

(*)   "The Great Turk leaves the Christians free to elect
and depose their pastors. If the Church in France were in the
same condition, we should have the liberty, we do not now
possess, of electing, deposing and assembling our pastors."
(Oeuvres de Fénelon, ed F. Didot, 1861, t. III, p. 432.)

cial re-organization arose, there had been found
an episcopate to recall to the world that the
solution of the problem should be sought in
the Gospel and in Catholic doctrine, instead
of seeking it in *l'Esprit des Lois* (*) and in
the *Contrat Social?* If the Church had spoken
with her authority in all questions where the
welfare of humanity was at stake, what light
would she not have shed on the darkness of
the controversies touching the mission of the
State and of society? Think of the resources
the Church would have brought to all the
generous and sincere leaders who, at the beginning of the Revolution, dreamed of a free
and rejuvenated France under the aegis of
religion and under the authority of the king!
The nation would have had its political creed
to oppose to the innovators, and the divorce
which the sophists succeeded in bringing
about between religion and the friends of liberty would have had no reason to exist.
The espousal by the men of those days of
the false maxims of the Revolution was possible only because of the silence of the gagged
and powerless Church; it would have been
prevented by churchmen conscious of their
mission and enjoying the fullness of freedom.

(*) Esprit des Lois (The Spirit of Laws) written by
Montesquieu 1748, 14 years before the Contrat Social of Rousseau. Its political influence was worldwide. But on various
points he seriously misunderstood Catholic teaching, and the
Sorbonne drew up a list of passages from his writings that
seemed to call for censure (August 1752).

Since then, if I may use the expression, the Catholic Church has once more become herself. One might have thought that she slept at the time of the Revolution; but it was the sleep of Jesus in the bark shaken by the tempest. Her awakening, tardy though it may seem, has been all the more fruitful. A great intellectual and social movement is already under way in the ranks of the Church: it is the beginning of the great struggle, the greatest of all her struggles against the powers of darkness.

Let us not make the same mistake and be deceived by appearances. Our own atmosphere is not less charged than was that of the Revolution. I dare say that even the Revolution was not preceded by symptoms as formidable as those which now, under our eyes, seem to foreshadow a new catastrophe. In our day, we would not smile at the prediction of another Cazotte tracing, as he did at the end of the eighteenth century, a dark and hopeless picture of the future.

New awakening of Christian society.

But, let us not forget that the condition of the Christian world has been greatly changed in the course of a century. Then the revolutionary spirit was young, bubbling with life; its hands were filled with promises of endless happiness; it was master of the earth; all humanity welcomed it; the forces of social conservation surrendered to it. But to-day it is old and decrepit; its prevarication is as clear as the light of day; condemned by all thinking men, it is no longer anything but a superstition believed in only by mediocre minds. At that time the Catholic Church, mutilated and enslaved, was a captive whom the catastrophe found prostrate at the foot of the throne, awaiting her turn to mount the scaffold. To-day, freed and herself again, she rises a giant and faces Revolution, not only to defend the domains which still are hers but also to recover those of which she has been despoiled. She has shattered all the maxims of philosophism. She has recalled to life the Society of Jesus whose suppression had been forced on her (*). She has proclaimed the infallibility of her head. In 1832 and in 1864, she condemned the false doctrine of 1789. Finally, building again on the ruins of the city of lies, she has proclaimed in immortal encyclicals the Christian Constitution of States and the Magna Charta of the emancipation of labor.

Who will deny that to-day, as in the Middle Ages, the Catholic Church is the highest authority? She speaks to all humanity in an accent sweet and strong and all her own. And she alone can talk to mankind. Amid the universal crash of thrones and schools and

----

(*) The Society of Jesus was restored by Pius VII, August 7, 1814, by the Bull "Solicitudo Omnium Ecclesiarum."

doctrines, she is the one moral force which remains standing and her astonishing superiority is enhanced by the very depth of their fall. She has but to raise her voice and from all parts of the universe she is answered. To-day there is such a thing as Catholic thought, which measures all things by the rule of Christian truth, condemning what is opposed to it, accepting what is not hostile. Strong and respected, conscious of its power, it circulates from one end of the world to the other; no longer can any sophism withstand it. In sociology, in science, in art, in all manifestations of the intellectual and moral life of the people, Catholic thought asserts itself with increasing force and energy. It is not refuted because it is irrefutable; it is opposed only by the conspiracy of silence.

Nor is this all. Descending from the field of doctrine to that of action, the Catholic spirit has taken possession of public life. The Catholic battalions are re-organized; on every side, an army of laymen is rising. The people come to uphold their clergy; the rank and file of the faithful insist on sharing the struggle. How cheering it is, in time of trouble, to see the recruits rally about their banner! The work is indeed long and tedious, but nothing can prevent its accomplishment! It is going on in different countries—in Belgium, in Holland, in Catholic Germany, in Northern Italy; in other countries persecution must

act as a spur to the tardy ones. And he would
be blind indeed who would fail to see in the
fury and stubborness of persecutors the ex-
piring effort of iniquity!

The triumph of the Catholic cause is secure, even from a human point of view. To-
day, as at all critical stages of her growth, she
has displayed the same marvelous adaptability. Detaching her cause from that of any
class that might seek to identify itself with
her, she has answered them as she answered
the Jews, as she answered Feudalism, as she
answered all the ghosts of the past. She lets
the dead bury their dead and enters into compact with the twentieth century. She lays
out a course for the rising masses. It is not
the course of the Revolution—as her slander-
ers say—it is the program of the Gospel, the
program of St. Thomas of Aquin (*). It is
the welcoming of all by the Kingdom of God,
disregarding birth and wealth, considering
only merit and virtue; it is the democracy of
the Gospel built upon the poor, and where we
see realized the law of justice and fraternity
in an ever widening application of the great
New Commandment.

She opposes to the bloody and sinister
ideals of the red flag and the cap of the con-

(*) How the principles of St. Thomas furnish a remedy for the evils affecting modern society is explained in the
great encyclicals of Leo XIII on the Christian constitution
of states, human liberty, the chief duties of Christians as citizens, and the condition of the working classes.

vict her incomparable ideal of the love of God
and the love of man, with its symbol of the
Cross. Despite all contrary appearances we
need not doubt of her final triumph. The
human soul is naturally Christian; everything great and good gravitates towards the
Gospel. Human society is drawn instinctively
in the direction of Jesus Christ whenever it
obeys the laws of self-preservation. The spirit
of evil may do its worst, it will but precipi-
tate events and hasten the day when humanity
will have choice only between Catholic civilization and revolutionary anarchy. And then
the choice will soon be made.

Let us then greet with hope and respect the
progress that is going on at this moment in
Christian society. It is a new Catholic
springtime. We have seen other spectacles
of the kind in our study of the Church in the
past. They must help us to appreciate what
is now going on under our eyes, affording, as
they do, a new proof of the indefectible vitality of the Church. We would indeed be blind
to the teachings of history were we, at this
stage of her life, to forget that now, as in the
past, she is upholding not the interests of a
class but the cause of humanity.

INDEX

INDEX—Continued

INDEX—Continued

INDEX—Continued

INDEX—Continued.

BOOKLIST.

Betten:
    The Ancient World.

Betten:
    The Modern World.

Stebbing:
    The Story of the Catholic Church.

Fouard:
    (Several volumes).

Allard:
    Ten Lectures on the Martyrs.

Moran:
    The Government of the Church In the First Centuries.

Battifol:
    Primitive Catholicism.

Rivere:
    The Expansion of Christianity In the First Three Centuries.

Montalambert:
    The Monks of the West.

Newman:
    Historical Sketches.

Grisar:
    Lives of the Popes.

Mann:
    Lives of the Popes.

Pastor:
    Lives of the Popes.

Gasquet:
    (Several volumse).

Walsh:
    The Thirteenth, the Greatest of Centuries.
    The Century of Columbus.

Baudrillart:
    The Catholic Church, the Renaissance and Protestantism.

Stone:
    Reformation and Renaissance.

Parsons:
    Studies in Church History.

Lilly:
    Christianity and Modern Civilization.

Devas:
    The Key to the Worlds' Progress.

Fortesque:
    The tOrthodox Eastern Church.
    The Lesser Eastern Churches.

Duchesne:
    The Churches Separated From Rome.

Cram:
    (Several volumes, especially):
    The Great Thousand Years.
    The Heart of Europe.
    The Substance of Gothic.

Devos:
    The Three Ages of Progress.

The books of above list are recommended by Rev. Wm. Busch, professor of history in the Seminary of St. Paul.

WHAT ARE THE MIDDLE AGES?

By
GODFREY KURTH

Authorized Translation from the Seventh French Edition
By
RT. REV. VICTOR DAY

Revised and Annotated Edition, 1924
Third Thousand

Copyright 1921
RT. REV. VICTOR DAY

NAEGELE PRINTING CO., HELENA, MONT.

Nihil Obstat
J. C. WILLGING
Censor

Imprimatur
JOANNES P. CARROLL
Episcopus Helenensis
In festo Praesentationis B. M. V. A. D. 1924

GENERAL ANALYTICAL INDEX

WHAT ARE THE MIDDLE AGES?

The current definition of the Middle Ages implies that they are an intermediary epoch between two civilizations, and, therefore, only a break in the course of civilization.

There is no term about the definition of which there is more perfect agreement than "The Middle Ages". We are told that the Middle Ages are an intermediary period between antiquity and modern times. This is the definition given by all dictionaries, encyclopedias, textbooks and summaries. (1) The most erudite writers on medieval history give no other definition. No matter how they differ in their appreciation of the Middle Ages, they all agree in the definition, and with singular unanimity declare that the Middle Ages are an intermediary epoch.

Which are the two periods separated by this break of a thousand years known as the Middle Ages? We are told that they are the two great civilizations of history—the ancient and the modern; the ancient, the Greco-Roman, with its splendid unity of a world pacified beneath the standards of Rome; the modern, with the wonderful variety of its national groups and the untold wealth of its intellectual manifestations—two worlds equally impressive, equally wonderful. They tell us that between these two quite distinct periods there stretches the long span of ten centuries during which the ancient civilization was dead and the modern civilization was yet unborn. These ten centuries, in their estimation, constitute a zone of darkness separating the light of the Greco-Roman world from the light of

---

(1) What the author says of European historians is true of American authors as well. Thus we read in Webster's International Dictionary: "The Middle Ages, the period of time intervening between the decline of the Roman Empire (A. D. 476) and the revival of letters." (Translator's note.)

the Renaissance. (1) Note that the very definition
puts the Middle Ages outside the pale of civilization
and brands them as a **night of a thousand years.**

Let us see precisely in what consists the opposition thus formulated between the generally received
idea of the Middle Ages and that of civilization.
Which are the two civilizations separated by the
"darkness" of the Middle Ages?

The first, of course, is the pagan civilization.
With slavery as its foundation and Caesarism as its
keystone, unable to satisfy the higher aspirations of
the human soul, it offers all the enjoyment of life to
the privileged few who wallow in sensual pleasures,
but condemns the rest of humanity to slavery.

Which is the second or the modern civilization?
Certainly not the Christian civilization, for otherwise
the second period would not begin as late as the
end of the Middle Ages, which were thoroughly imbued with the Christian idea. On the contrary, this
second civilization is a civilization which reacts
against the Christian ideal by evoking the pagan
spirit from the ashes of the past and which, like
paganism, gives the despotism of Caesar as a code
to the State and the quest of pleasure as a law to
the individual. It is a recurrence of pagan civilization.

If, as most writers assert, the Middle Ages are
really an intermediary period, it is precisely because
this epoch enthrones the Christian ideal of mortifi-
cation and poverty between the first and second
periods of this pagan civilization. This aspect of
the Middle Ages makes the second civilization but a

----

(1) Renaissance, the intellectual movement in Europe
marked by a larger diffusion of classical learning and art in
Italy in the fifteenth century and the similar revival following in other countries. This movement resulted from the
gradual progress that had been going on during the Middle
Ages for a thousand years. See: "The Church at the Turning
Points of History" Kurth-Day, p. 123 (Tr. n.)

revival of the old civilization:—antiquity arises from the grave, again takes possession of the world, closes the parenthesis opened by the Middle Ages and begins anew the era of the great progress of humanity! This view of the Middle Ages would regard Christianity as nothing but an eclipse after whose passing men again walk the road of free scientific research and taste again the great aesthetic joys of life. The Renaissance virtually puts an end to Christianity. Civilization, paganism, and the Renaissance become synonyms just as barbarism, Christianity, and the Middle Ages are synonymous.

The current definition of the Middle Ages has created a misconception of the Middle Ages.

Thus, the definition of the Middle Ages, as we have recorded it without comment, is a definition with a double meaning. It implies more than would appear at first sight.

I do not say that the definition carries its full significance to the minds of those who use it, nor that the mere term "Middle Ages", whenever uttered, calls forth all the ideas which it connotes and without which it would be meaningless. Very frequently the words we use are merely conventional formulas whose real significance is not discerned, and which often convey quite the opposite of their true meaning.

This does not mean that in this given case the word has had no influence upon the idea. The word in question presents, or seems to present, an obvious meaning and this meaning becomes definite only when we oppose to the idea of the Middle Ages the idea of the two civilizations which it separates. This opposition led logically to the inference that medieval society was barbarous. Thus there arose a general prejudice against the people of the Middle Ages. As a whole they were considered coarse, barbarous, ignorant, dull, filthy, the dupes of crafty priests and of their own prejudices, either the subjects or the authors of all kinds of violence, incapable of public spirit, utterly unable to rise to the grand ideas of country, progress, social justice, and intellectual life.

Hence the many depressing legends which constitute the sum total of knowledge possessed by men of former centuries and by many of our own time concerning the Middle Ages. Picture to yourself what an encyclopedist of a hundred years ago thought of the Middle Ages, what certain belated followers of Voltaire think of them to the present day. Can one imagine a sadder, a more repugnant, a more hateful picture?

Let us look deeper into the matter. The encyclopedists of a hundred years ago and the belated followers of Voltaire say that the reign of Christianity began with the burning of the library of Alexandria, (1) which destroyed the intellectual patrimony of humanity, and that it came to a close with the funeral pyres of the Inquisition, (2) which burned those who endeavored to restore that patrimony.

---

(1)   The Library of Alexandria founded about 284 B. C. contained, according to some historians, seven hundred thousand papyrus rolls (books). On the capture of the city by matter of the library to Caliph Omar and received the matter of the library to the Caliph Omar and received the answer: "If these writings of the Greeks agree with the book of God, (Koran, or the sacred book of the Mohammedans) they are useless and need not be preserved; if they disagree, they are pernicoius, and ought to be destroyed." (Tr. n.)

(2)   The Inquisition. The early Christian State was not indifferent to the admixture of error with the Christain religion. Starting from this viewpoint the Christian Roman Emperor Theodosius II, A. D. 407, declared heresy to be also a crime against the State, and threatened obstinate defenders of the heresies condemned by the Church with such punishments as imprisonment, banishment, confiscation of property, and in some cases even with death. This led to the establishment of the Ecclesiastical Inquisition and later of the Spanish Inquisition. The duty of the secular power to punish heretics was still recognized in the sixteenth century, by Catholics and Protestants alike. It is acknowledged by nobody today. (Tr. n.)

These same persons hold that, between these two conflagrations, in the grewsome twilight reddened by their flames and screened by their smoke, we observe that succession of distressing pictures which have earned for the Middle Ages the contempt of all friends of humanity.

What a horrible spectacle is thus presented to us! They would have us believe that during those ages a council gravely discussed whether or not woman has a soul; and that one of the sex, no doubt to retaliate on an ungallant episcopacy, succeeded in mounting the chair of Peter.

They would have us believe that at the very time the papacy was guilty of such scandal it worked with the greatest zeal at forging false titles. According to them, the papacy, during the eighth century, forged the "Donation of Constantine" (1) and, in the ninth century, fabricated the False Decretals (2) in order to further establish its title to the pretended donation.

They represent the Church authorities enslaving and brutalizing the nations, for centuries winking at

---

(1) Donation of Constantine. By this name is understood, since the end of the Middle Ages, a forged document of Emperor Constantine the Great (A. D. 337) by which large privileges and rich possessions were conferred on the Pope and the Roman Church. This document is without doubt a forgery, fabricated somewhere between the years 750 and 850. (Tr. n.)

(2) False Decretals, or the Decretals of the Pseudo-Isidore, is a name given to certain apocryphal papal letters contained in a collection of canon laws, compiled about the middle of the ninth century, by an author who uses the pseudonym of Isidore Mercator. For the past four hundred years the opponents of the Papacy have asserted that its power and authority from the Middle Ages onward were based chiefly on the "False Decretals." The Church heard the charge with the greatest equanimity, for she knew full well that Papal claims could be proved independently of the forged documents. In 1914 Mr. Davenport, an English Protestant lawyer, took up the cudgels for the Church, and won the Lothian prize at Oxford with an essay on the "False Decretals" in which he refutes the inaccurate statements of many anti-Catholic writers on the subject. (Tr. n.)

the infamous "right of the lord", and not opposing
the custom of the lords who returning from the
hunt were wont to slash open the stomachs of their
tenants to take a warm footbath.

This dismal picture of the Middle Ages represents a helpless and stupified people whose only hope
was the frightful expectation of the Last Judgment:
they looked for the end of the world in the year One
Thousand, and were quite surprised that the end of
that year found the world still existing.

In the shadows of this same picture we see the
people—innocent victims of an avaricious and fanatical clergy—dragged for centuries to the far off
butcheries of the Orient, bringing back leprosy as
the only reward for their exploits (1). And we are
told further that even this terrible plague was
powerless to teach them cleanliness, that during the
entire Middle Ages our ancestors wallowed in dis-
gusting filth, for Michelet says that the people had
not a bath for a thousand years.

And to add more gloom to the picture they tell
us that the people were without the consolations
which intellectual life affords. They assure us that
there was no science and that the people were with-

----

(1) The Crusades were expeditions into the Mohammedan lands, undertaken by the Christian nations of western
Europe, at the suggestion of the Popes, to insure protection
to the Christian pilgrims to the Holy Land and to rescue the
Holy Sepulcher of Christ from the Mohammedans. The Crusades put a stop to the incessant wars of petty princes,
saved Europe from conquest by the Turk, prolonged the life
of the Eastern Empire for four centuries, led to the establishment of trade relations with the Eastern peoples, gave a
new impetus to the sciences and arts of Western Europe,
gave the Communes and the serfs a chance to buy their freedom from their lords and masters, procured the crown of
martyrdom for millions of Christian heroes, secured protection for pilgrims to the Holy Land and rescued, at least for
a time, the Holy Sepulchre from the Turks. The Crusader
stands forever as the type of the soldier who fights for a high
and noble ideal; hence the American Expeditionary Forces
in France in the World War were called "Pershing's Crusaders." (Tr. n.)

out schools, as it was to the interest of the Church
to maintain ignorance; that there was no intellectual
effort, no philosophy, as all spontaneous mental activity was considered a sin against faith.   They
would have us believe that the Middle Ages were
without art excepting, of course, certain monuments
which, they claimed, came from the Arabians and
whose barbarism was best expressed by coining the
word "Gothic". We are told that there was no
poetry: Boileau himself repeats this in his "Art
Poetique" where he asserts that poetry was unknown
until Villon disentangled the involved art of our
ancient romancers and that the theater was a pleasure
unknown to our devout ancestors (1).   Finally,
Malherbe came (2).   And after Malherbe followed
Erasmus (3) and Luther (4) and the Humanists (5)

----

(1) Boileau-Despréaux, Nicholas, French poet, satirist
and critic (1636-1711), best known by his "Art Poétique" in
which he gives the history and lays down, in verse, the rules
of poetic composition in the French langauge. (Tr. n.)

(2) Francois de Malherbe, French poet, born in 1555,
died in 1628. (Tr. n.)

(3) Erasmus, Desiderius Erasmus of Rotterdam was the
most celebrated humanist of his time, a man of great learning but destitute of nobility of character, and of uncertain
disposition. He was first the friend, then the opponent of
Luther. He died in Basle A. D. 1536. By his edition of the
"Fathers of the Church" he rendered great service to patris-
tic literature. (Tr. n.)

(4) Luther, born in Eisleben, Saxony, A. D. 1483, became
an Augustinian monk in 1505. In 1508 he was made professor of philosophy at Wittenberg. On October 31, 1517, he
affixed his famous ninety-five theses to the door of the castle
church of Wittenberg. This action inaugurated the movement known as the Protestant Reformation, which rejected
the authority of the Pope, Transubstantiation, etc., taught the
doctrine of justification by faith alone, that man is wholly
corrupted by the Fall, and that the Bible is the sole rule of
faith. (Tr. n.)

(5) Humanism is the name given to the intellectual,
literary, and scientific movement of the fourteenth, fifteenth
and sixteenth centuries, a movement which aimed at basing
every branch of learning on the literature and culture of
classical antiquity. Believing that a classical training alone
could form a perfect man, the followers of this movement
called themselves "Humanists". (Tr. n.)

and the Reformers, who, in the common estimation, were the saviors to lead our ancestors back to the traditional paths of civilization.

Refutation of legends concerning the Middle Ages.

More than one of our contemporaries have still to learn that long ago science disposed of this dark aspect of the Middle Ages. The pitiless hand of criticism has forever demolished the edifice of fable built up since the time of the Renaissance, chiefly by the selfstyled philosophers of the eighteenth century. A cursory review of the answers made by criticism to the assertions of Voltaire (1) and of the "Encyclopedists" (2) will be a pleasant diversion.

The Myth of the Soulless Woman.

If there is any fable which lays bare the folly of its peddlers, it is certainly that which represents the Council of Macon discussing the question of the soul of woman. It would be an offense to the intelligence of my readers if I thought it necessary to state that this question was never raised in Christian society, either at the Council of Macon, or elsewhere. At

---

(1) Voltaire, Francois, Arouet de (1694-1778), a French writer who devoted his versatile talents to reviving the calumnies of the Roman pagan writer Celsus against the Apostles and the first Christians, and to popularizing the religious errors of the Freethinkers of England. Luther had cherished a violent hatred against the Vicar of Christ. Voltaire bore such a hatred against Christ hmiself. His watchword was "Ecrasez l' Infâme" (Crush the Infamous viz. Christ and Christianity). One of his favorite maxims was: "Lie! Lie! my friends, and something will be sure to stick." (Tr. n.)

(2) The Encyclopedists were the writers of the "Encyclopédie," a work in twenty-eight folio volumes published in French between 1751 and 1772, under the direction of Diderot (1713-1784). The aim of the Encyclopédie in religious matters was the rejection of all Christian dogma. (Tr. n.)

the Council of Macon there was a bishop—somewhat
of a purist—who took exception to the word "man"
as applied to woman. But they convinced him that
his scruple as to grammar was unfounded, since
Scripture itself more than once uses the word in
this meaning. This is the whole story, and we may
award a dunce-cap to any one who thinks he knows
more than this about it (1).

Popess Joan.

It would be even more preposterous today to
peddle the story of the Popess Joan (2). Should a
present-day writer with any pretention to erudition
undertake to refute this fable, he would offend all
intelligent authors and be looked upon as one out of
date and wasting precious time.

We put aside these two anecdotes which a century ago "strong minds" used as "terrible argu-
ments" against the Catholic faith and pass on to
more serious questions.

Donation of Constantine.

It is claimed that it was the papacy that invented
the story of the "Donation of Constantine". We

---

(1) Godfrey Kurth, "Le Concile de Macon et les
femmes," in "La Revue des questions historiques", vol. LI.,
April, 1892.

Very Rev. Charles Aiken, S. T. D., in "The Catholic
World" of March, 1918.

See also "America" in the following numbers: March
24, 1915; January 9, 1916; January 22, 1916; March 11, 1916;
March 18, 1916; and March 25, 1916. (Tr. n.)

(2) Popess Joan is supposed to have occupied the Chair
of Peter from 855 to 857 according to one "authority", and
about 1100 according to another "authority", whilst the fable
is first noticed in literature in the middle of the thirteenth
century. But the legendary person does not fit in at either
time, because at both times the Chair of Peter was occupied
by well known Popes. This matter is treated at length in
"The Catholic World" for September, 1914, in "The Legend
of Pope Joan" by Rev. Bertrand L. Conway, C. S. P.

admit that "The Donation of Constantine" is a
legend. It is a pious legend, which aims to account
for the origin of the Temporal Power of the Pope by
connecting it with the first Christian Emperor, just
as the Romans of the Republic connected all their
military and religious institutions with their first
kings, Romulus and Numa Pompilius. But to pretend that this legend was invented by the **Papacy** in
order to establish its title, is to show absolute ignorance of the Catholic philosophy of law; for, being in
uncontested possession of the sovereignty of fact
from time immemorial, the Papacy had, by that very
fact, a title, namely, that of prescription with the
tacit consent of the nations. But even were it otherwise, this charge against the Papacy should be supported at least by a shadow of proof. But no proof
is offered, the charge is gratuitous, rash, and unjust
to the Papacy; it has no foundation, and we have
the right to ignore it.

False Decretals.

And the False Decretals? Has not e n o u g h
printer's ink been wasted on that subject, and have
not a sufficient number of contradictory solutions
been invented? Almost every year the question is
again up for discussion and a new birthplace is
assigned to this notorious apocryphal collection. Of
late Rheims and Le Mans have been mentioned most
frequently, and no doubt still other towns will be
named; but curiously enough Rome has not yet been
suggested. Of course, the question of place is not
very important, and if it were really proven that
the authority of the Roman Pontiffs in the Church
rests on an apocryphal document we could only
blush and hang our heads in shame. But, far from
this being the case, the documents themselves prove
the contrary, because they invoke the authority of
the Popes themselves to withdraw the bishops from

the jurisdiction of their metropolitan and subject them directly to the Holy See. The "False Decretals," far from giving authority to the Popes, presuppose that authority. (1)

The Right of the Lord.

Now we come to the infamous accusation that for centuries the feudal lords enjoyed, in the case of young married women of their vassalage, a right so revolting that pagan antiquity had never heard of such a thing and would have branded the abuse with indignation had it b e e n known. Moreover, t h i s charge implies that the Catholic Church, which has always considered virginity as the most gl~.ious title of the two sexes, which condemns even a look or a thought contrary to chastity, which has fought countless fights ~gainst kings and lords of this world in defense of the inviolability of the conjugal tie, would have winked at a practice which made of man a brute and of woman a prey. The Church would have kept a cowardly silence in presence of adultery raised to the dignity of a public institution for the benefit of a few lewd lords! But this consideration has not stopped the wretches from repeating this lowest and vilest of calumnies. Unfortunately for them, the works of Louis Veuillot and Karl Schmidt have so shattered this legend that one cannot repeat it without risking one's reputation. (2)

Warm Blood Bath.

We need merely mention the legend of the warm blood bath which, upon his return from the hunt, the

---

(1) "The Catholic World" for August, 1917, or "False Decretals" by Bertrand L. Conway, C. S. P., published in pamphlet form by The Paulist Press, New York. (Tr. n.)

(2) See Louis Veuillot, "Le droit du seigneur au moyen age", Paris, 1854, and Karl Schmidt, "Jus primae noctis", Fribourg, 1881.

lord was supposed to have taken in the entrails of his tenants. The legend has had but a restricted circulation, and the common sense of readers has refused it credence.

The Terrors of the Year One Thousand.

We now come to the supposed terrors of the year One Thousand. Public credulity fell a victim to this legend. The readers of the nineteenth century believed in these so-called terrors as unanimously as their ancestors are supposed to have experienced them. Well, it is established to-day that the Terrors of the Year One Thousand are nothing but a legend made up by the writers of the seventeenth and eighteenth centuries, chiefly by Robertson, in the introduction to his "History of Charles V". As this work has enjoyed great popularity, every one repeats the legend on the authority of Robertson, without thinking of verifying it. In an article of the "Revue des Questions Historiques" published in 1873, Dom Plain had but to blow upon the fabrication of Robertson to dissipate it into thin air. Since then, several historians of renown have repeated and completed the demonstration of Dom Plain. The case has been heard and decided. Henceforth there will be no more question of the year One Thousand in our textbooks of history.

Leprosy.

Do you really think that "historians" will not write again of the Terrors of the Year One Thousand? I fear I have made a rash statement in saying so, for, if there is a truth attested by experience, it is the good nature with which, in historiography, authors continue religiously to repeat to new generations errors long since disposed of by science. This reminds us of the stars which according to the astronomers have disappeared ages ago, and which, nevertheless, still send their light to globes scattered in endless space. The history of leprosy supplies a proof of this tender solicitude of certain writers for legends that have gone out of fashion. Does not every one know, do not all writers repeat, that leprosy was brought to the West by the Crusaders after the eleventh century? Now, fourteen years ago, I established in the most peremptory manner the falsity of this legend, and I showed that, down from the fourth century, leprosy was spread throughout all the lands of western Europe; that, from the fourth to the twelfth century, it existed, without interruption; that Church and State and private charity gave it attention; that the Church councils and the civil governments enacted laws concerning it; that there existed numerous lazar-houses; and, finally, that there is not the slightest evidence that the Crusades even contributed to increase the number of lepers. (1) But in spite of my demonstration to the contrary, ''historians'', even in specialized works, continue to repeat that leprosy was introduced into Western Europe by the Crusades. My readers may acquaint themselves with the proofs of the above facts by consulting my paper on the subject.

No Baths in a Thousand Years.

But really it was not necessary to blame leprosy on the Crusades, since a more direct and permanent cause could have been alleged, namely, the ''horrible filth'' prevailing during that epoch. In fact, Michelet did not overlook the opportunity. (2) According to him, leprosy was due to the fact that people

---

(1) G. Kurth, "La lèpre en Occident avant les Croisades," in "Report of the Second International Scientific Congress of Catholics, Section 5, Paris, 1891."

(2) Michelet, Jules, French historian and miscellaneous writer (1798-1874). (Tr. n.)

did not wash during the Middle Ages: "Not a bath
in a thousand years!" (He forgets the warm blood
baths!) The beautiful stereotyped formula of Michelet was well calculated to inoculate shallow minds
with the doctrines of the author, but proves to be
a boomerang to his memory, since it convicts him
of unpardonable levity. Has there not been enough
idle talk on this foolish statement? Indeed it is well
established that during the Middle Ages baths were
among the most popular and universal institutions,
that there was not a town however small that did
not have its public baths, (1) and that, on the contrary, it was the Renaissance which permitted the
habits of cleanliness of the Middle Ages gradually
to fall into desuetude, substituting for them a negli-
gence which degenerated into the most repulsive un-
cleanliness. (2) We can but pity those who are
ignorant of these well established facts and who to
the present day peddle stories so thoroughly discredited in history.

These considerations show that the Middle Ages
of legend cannot withstand the Middle Ages of history. Not wishing to prolong an enumeration which
might be continued almost indefinitely, I have confined myself to these specimens of rectification for
the benefit of those who know the past only from
their readings of the "Encyclopedie" or its trailers.

*Criticism of the current definition of the
term "Middle Ages." This definition is taken
from philology and has a meaning entirely
different from the one contemptuously attributed to it.*

But no rectification of details, even when they
are important, can do away with the false ideas

(1)   Lecoy de la Marche: "Les bains" in "La Société au
XIII Siècle," Paris, 1880.
(2)   Enlart. Manuel d'archéologie francaise, vol. ii, p. 95.
See Rt. Rev. Thomas J. Shahan in "The Middle Ages"
on "Baths and Bathing in the Middle Ages," p. 290, ff. (Tr. n.)

concerning the Middle Ages, so long as people persist in considering them as a break between two periods of civilization. Since this error is altogether due to the definition, I shall show how that definition is deceiving and without foundation.

I remark first that the definition is entirely verbal, and consists of puerile tautology. All that the definition teaches is that the Middle Ages are middle ages. This seems to imply little enough, but it was not all that the term conveyed to the minds of those who created it. In its primitive acceptance the expression had quite a different meaning from that given it today; and I claim that, as applied to the first ten centuries, this meaning is wrong and almost misleading. I now offer proofs for my contention.

History is a relatively recent science; it is only of late that it has acquired a method of its own, and has freed itself from philology, of which it was a part up to the sixteenth century. Therefore we should not be surprised that the historians, who followed after the philologists, should have borrowed from them their terminology, and carried into the domain of historical studies words which lost their meaning in crossing the border line. The term in question is a striking instance of the disadvantages resulting from such borrowing.

In studying the development of the Latin tongue, from its origin down to their own time, the philologists had noticed its several periods, and had given each a name. The first period was that of the classical Latin, which witnessed the birth of the masterpieces of Roman literature, and during which the Latin language was spoken by all the people who partook of the Roman civilization. The second period was that of the barbarian Latin. When the Roman civilization p e r i s h e d in Western Europe,

(1) the Latin language was inherited by the Germanic peoples who were strangers to its genius and who, intermingled with the Roman populations, gradually learned the Latin tongue but disfigured it in divers ways in the various countries in which they lived, so that Latin as spoken by them became a new language. Finally, there came a period when these neo-Latin languages, now definitely fixed, became the only language of the people, whilst the Latin, left to the men of learning, existed thenceforth in books only, and became a dead language.

The first of these periods, as commonly accepted, extended from the beginning of the Roman State down to the reign of Constantine the Great. (2) Indeed it was under the administration of this prince that the Barbarians first flocked in compact masses into the Empire to serve it until they might enslave it. The second period extended to the reign of

---

(1) In 476 the Latin Empire of the West ceased to be, and its rich provinces became the prey of the Germanic tribes. Great Britain was conquered by the Anglo-Saxons, Gaul by the Franks and Burgundians, Spain by the Visigoths and the Suevi, Italy by the Ostrogoths and the Lombards, and Africa by the Vandals. (Tr. n.)

(2) Constantine the Great, son of Constantine Chlorus, joint emperor with Galerius, in 312 marched upon Maxentius, the worthless ruler of Rome. One day, shortly after noontime, while pondering on the heavy odds that were against him, he and the soldiers who happened to be with him beheld a fiery cross in the sky with this inscription: "In touto nika" (In this conquer). During the following night Christ, in a vision, told him to approach the enemy under the standard of the cross. This Constantine did. The new standard, called "Labarum", preceded his host in the battle at the Milvian Bridge. Maxentius suffered a crushing defeat, and was drowned in the Tiber. Constantine publicly ascribed the victory to the God of the Christians, and embraced the Christian faith, in which he was later baptized. In 313, Constantine, together with Licinius, his ally, issued the famous edict of Milan by which full liberty was granted to the Christians. This event marks the beginning of a new era for Christianity, for the Roman Empire, and for the world at large. The victory of Christianity at this time and the subsequent general conversion of the Empire's population, made possible the conversion and civilization of the Barbarians, who were to conquer the Empire politically. (Tr. n.)

Charlemagne (1).   During this period the Latin tongue fell under the control of the Barbarians, became the instrument of their culture and the vehicle of their general ideas, until the advent of the modern languages. The third period began after the death of Charlemagne, and witnessed the birth of the modern languages. It heard their first stammerings in the oath of Strasburg (A. D. 842) (2) and assisted successively at the births of the various neo-Latin tongues of all Europe.

To each of these three ages of the Latin tongue

---

(1)   Charlemagne (742-814), King of the Franks, first sovereign of the Christian Empire of the West, was a great patron of letters. Under his reign, notwithstanding his continual wars, he established schools throughout his empire. He invited Alcuin (A. D. 804), a distinguished English scholar and pupil of the Venerable Bede, and under his direction establisred academies. The sons of the more wealthy flocked to his lectures. Alcuin spoke Latin, Greek, and Hebrew, was master of philosophy, theology, history, and mathematics. Under his supervision the schools of the empire became celebrated, and scholars from all Europe came to learn wisdom at his feet. The impulse thus given to letters by Charlemagne was continued by his successors. The statues of Constantine the Great and Charlemagne grace the vestibule of the basilica of St. Peter in Rome. (Tr. n.)

(2)   The Oath of Strasburg is the earliest extant specimen of the French language. In 842, in the presence of their assembled armies at Strasburg, Charles the Bald and Louis the Germanic, grandsons of Charlemagne, took this solemn oath of friendship and fidelity, forming an alliance against their eldest brother Lothaire. The oath was made in German to the German army by Charles the Bald, King of the West Franks, and in early French to the West Franks by Louis the Germanic, and is preserved in both languages. It might be interesting to quote the opening words of the oath both in early German and in early French. To show the gradual evolution of modern French from the Latin tongue during the Middle Ages, we add to the early French both Latin and modern French translations:

Latin: Pro Dei amore et pro christiani populi et nostra communi salute.

Early French: Pro Deo amur et pro christian poblo et nostro commun salvament.

Modern French: Pour l'amour de Dieu et pour le salut du peuple chrétien et notre salut commun.

German: In Godes minna ind in thes christianes folches ind unser bedhere gehaltnissi.

English: For God's love and for the salvation of the Christian people and our common salvation. (Tr. n.)

the philologists had given a name to mark its proper place in the development of the language. The first age was naturally called the high or superior age; the second, the middle age; the third, the inferior or low age. Thus the term "Middle Ages", according to its etymology and in its primitive acceptance, designated nothing else than a period of latinity extending between the reigns of Constantine the Great and Charlemagne. This was the meaning ascribed to it by the Humanists, also by Ducange when he gave to his celebrated dictionary the title "Glossarium mediæ et infimæe latinitatis". (Dictionary of Middle and Low Latin) (1)

In borrowing the term "Middle Ages" from the philologists, and transferring it to the domain of historiography, the historians at first did not modify its meaning. They adopted both the name and the period which it covered and designated as the "Middle Ages" that historical and political period which intervened between Constantine the Great and Charlemagne. The entire period subsequent to Charlemagne, they designated as the "aetas infima", or "low age". It is now known as the modern epoch.

But while the historians were adopting the language of the philologists, the Humanists were extending the limits they had at first assigned to their "Middle Ages". They began to look upon their time as a fourth and new age of latinity. They loved to think that, under the magic influence of their pen, the Latin tongue had been regenerated and restored to its pristine purity, and they saw in the period beginning with the sixteenth century a new phase of latinity which marked its second birth, or renaissance. Thenceforth they united the second and third periods, both of which had marked the decline of

---

(1) Ducange, Charles du Fresne, French historian and philologist. (1610-1688) (Tr. n.)

the Latin tongue, and called them the **middle** period.
Thus they extended the middle ages of the Latin
language to a period stretching from the decline
of the Roman Empire under Constantine the Great
to the Renaissance.

And again the historians followed in the footsteps of the philologists. They took the ten Christian centuries which the philologists marked as blank
in regard to latinity—itself a debatable matter—and
marked them as blank also as regards civilization.
The exchange of terms brought about the exchange
of viewpoints, and confusion of ideas resulted from
the confusion of words.

Thus the term "Middle Ages" in its present acceptance, fraudulently passed into the language of
historiography; it cannot furnish a regular birth
certificate, for it is the offspring of a confusion of
ideas.

*First uses of the term "Middle Ages" in
its present sense.*

It is not my task to determine when the term
"Middle Ages" was first used in its present sense.
I find that in 1639 it was already a part of the regu-
lar vocabulary. (1)

However, strictly speaking, I do not hold historians responsible for the misunderstanding. The
pedagogues are the real culprits. The desire to
classify is a characteristic trait of the schoolman.
Thus, it was a professor, Christopher Keller, better
known by his latinized name, Cellarius, who first
used the term in the title of a textbook (A. D.
1688). (2)

Another schoolman, Loescher, introduced t h e
word into a German work published in the year

----

(1)   Rausin of Liège in "Leodium," p. 103.

(2)   Chr. Cellarii "Historia Medii Aevi, a temporibus
Constantini Magni ad Constantinopolim a Turcis captam
deducta." Iena 1688.

1725; since then the expression has been in constant use in pedagogical works and gradually found its way into literary productions.

But not before the second half of the eighteenth century does the term appear in literary works. And the great writers of that epoch, in France as well as in Germany, use it seldom and with hesitancy. The French Academy did not admit the term into the official repertoire of the language until the publication of the sixth edition of its dictionary, in 1835. (1)

I think that the above considerations utterly discredit the common definition of the designation "Middle Ages".

The Middle Ages are not an intermediary period; on the contrary, they are the beginning of modern society.

But it may be contended that in spite of its etymology the term "Middle Ages" is the appropriate name of an intermediary epoch.

Such a contention is false, and cannot be justified from an historical viewpoint. Far from being intermediary between the ancient and the modern civilizations, the "Middle Ages" are the beginning of modern civilization. This modern civilization did not begin with the epoch of the Renaissance but is the offspring of Christianity, and we must seek its cradle as near as possible to the crib of Bethlehem. It began when the pagan civilization of Rome collapsed. On the ruins of pagan civilization new socie-

---

(1) The French Academy is a national institution of France, founded by Cardinal de Richelieu in 1635. It is composed of forty members popularly called the "Immortals". The object for which the Academy was founded was the purification of the French language. To attain this end it compiled a dictionary. The office of the Academy is not to create words, but to register words approved by the authority of the best writers and by good society. (Tr. n.)

ties were built which were Christian in principle, if not in their material elements.

These societies still stand on their original foundation, Christian morality. They were begun during the centuries of the Middle Ages and continued to flourish during subsequent centuries. We are the heirs of the Middle Ages, not, as some would have it, the heirs of Greece and Rome. But in our study of the classics our views in this matter are apt to become so distorted that it is necessary to verify an evident truth.

We offer the following proof of our position:

Whatever is lasting and fruitful in modern society, regarding institutions and ideas, has its roots deep in the fertile soil of the first Christian centuries.

The Middle Ages put an end to ancient slavery and called all men to freedom. To loosen link by link the chain of slavery was the work of centuries. It resulted in the most positive accomplishment of modern civilization.

The Middle Ages rent the imperial unity of the world and substituted the m o d e r n nationalities. These nationalities still exist, and the twentieth century has no higher task than to guard their welfare and foster their friendly relations.

The Middle Ages created the modern languages, and thereby gradually eliminated the Latin. These are the languages which we speak today and which hold unprecedented e m i n e n c e in the world of thought.

The Middle Ages accepted the Christian Faith with love and defended it on every battlefield and with every weapon. Is not the Christian faith the queen of the world to the present day? Has any non-Christian conception of the universe been embodied in an organization as glorious as the Church, or here below manifested itself by a more marvelous fecundity?

The Middle Ages made the Papacy the most respected institution of the world. Even in our own time the preeminence of the Papacy is undisputed.

The Middle Ages enforced the distinction between the temporal and the spiritual, the great principle which flows from the Gospel, and which in the past has renovated and today upholds the political and social spirit of the civilized world.

The Middle Ages founded the constitutional monarchy and representative government, both unknown to antiquity, but which are indispensable conditions for the political existence of modern nations.

Under the shelter of these public liberties, which were guaranteed by covenant between prince and subject, the Middle Ages gave impetus to all forms of association, from the municipal corporation down to the labor union, and bequeathed to us models to which, in spite of the storms of revolution, humanity unceasingly turns for imitation.

The art of the Middle Ages has become our art. The name Gothic, (1) which was applied to the architecture of the Middle Ages as a term of contempt, is bestowed on our art as a title of glory and to-day we draw inspiration from the very words which our predecessors despised.

(1) The word Gothic designates the style of architecture which flourished in the western part of Europe from the end of the twelfth century to the revival of the classical styles in the sixteenth century. Generally speaking, it is at once the most scientific and the most artistic style of architecture. It is the most scientific because its whole strength is made to reside in a finely organized and frankly confessed framework rather than in walls. This framework, made up of piers, arches and buttresses, is freed from every unnecessary incumbrance of wall and is rendered as light in all its parts as is compatible with strength. It is the most artistic style because the liberal, harmonious and consistent use of the pointed arch, the trefoil, the quatrefoil, the cinquefoil, foliated capitals, deep mouldings, finials, crockets, four-leaved flowers, etc., enable the artist to make Gothic buildings pictures of perfect beauty. (Tr. n.)

The poets of the seventeenth and eighteenth centuries gloried in their ignorance of the national poetry of the Middle Ages; we love it, we admire it, we have given it our undying affection. Littre has shown how unjust is the contemptuous attitude of Boileau towards the literature of the Middle Ages. (1)

And we shall not have surpassed the Middle Ages until we shall have erected a more beautiful cathedral than that of Rheims, (2) painted a more inspiring canvas than the picture of the Adoration of the Lamb, (3) and written a poem more powerful than the Divina Commedia (4). All that we

---

(1) Littré, Maximilien Paul Emile. French philologist (1801-1881). (Tr. n.)

(2) The Cathedral of Rheims is called the national cathedral of France, whose kings were consecrated within its sacred precincts. The first stone of the present structure was laid in 1212, the main front with its superb towers was completed in 1427. The Cathedral of Rheims is considered by many the most perfect specimen of decorated Gothic architecture in existence on account of the symmetry of its proportions, the purity of its style, the gracefulness of its lines, the wealth of its sculptural decorations numbering two thousand five hundred statues, six hundred of which grace the main entrance. (Tr. n.)

(3) The Adoration of the Lamb painted by Hubert Van Eyck and John Van Eyck, his brother, Belgian painters, between 1420 and 1432. It is now in the cathedral of St. Bavon of Ghent, Belgium. It is a polyptich, or painting of many panels, each one of which constitutes a group, and all of which make but one main subject. The Adoration of the Lamb is the pictorial representation of Apocalypse: "After this I saw a great multitude, which no man could number, of all nations, and tribes, and peoples, and tongues, standing before the throne, and in sight of the Lamb, clothed with white robes, and palms in their hands. And they cried with a loud voice, saying: Salvation to our God, who sitteth upon the throne, and to the Lamb" (Apoc., VII., 9-10). For a detailed description see: "Belgium: Its Cities". Vol. I, Grant Allen. Published by L. C. Page & Co., Boston. (Tr. n.)

(4) "Divina Commedia," written by Dante Alighieri, Italian poet, born at Florence, in 1265, and who died at Ravenna, Italy, September 14, 1321. His best known work is the "Divina Commedia", which lends the charm of poetry to the truths of religion, whilst leading the reader through Hell, Purgatory, and Heaven. This sacred poem sums up the knowledge and intellectual attainment of the Middle Ages, and places Dante among the few supreme poets of the world. (Tr. n.)

have—our religion and our political ideas, our nationality and our language, our aesthetics and our
social economy—all these connect us with the Middle Ages and separate us from antiquity. We are
the heirs of the Middle Ages; we continue their
work, not the work of the Renaissance.

The Renaissance is, in a certain sense, an intermediary period.

If there be any epoch to which we may apply
the term "Middle Ages", is it not the Renaissance
itself which opened in the history of modern nations
a parenthesis now closed or soon to be closed? The
idols of the Renaissance are now overthrown, and we
turn away from its ideal. We try to keep clear of
royal absolutism and of the centralization which is
its logical consequence. We utterly repudiate the
famous maxim of the sixteenth century "Cujus regio
ejus religio", the religion of the ruler must be the
religion of the kingdom, which maxim is but another
rendering of the Ulpian oracle, "Quod principi placuit
legis habet vigorem", whatever pleases the ruler has
the force of law. In matters of art and literature
we have formally broken with classicism and have
returned to the national traditions, to the sources
of popular and Christian inspiration. The modern
spirit repudiates that purely pagan conception of
life which would have the soul with all its faculties
gravitate towards the two poles of voluptuousness
and glory; the modern spirit offers as motive for
individual effort the sentiment of human solidarity
and disinterested love of social progress.

Over the head of the Renaissance we clasp hands
with our ancestors of the Middle Ages; we again
tread the paths from which we had been led astray
by the Renaissance.

Does this mean that we should meet one extreme with another by denying all indebtedness to the Renaissance and by casting away the contribution which the Renaissance has brought to the treasury of civilization? By no means! Humanity has no right to self-mutilation but must gratefully accept whatever is contributory to its intellectual and moral power. Now, the Renaissance is one of the most splendid intellectual phenomena of history; it developed such wealth of genius and enlarged the intellectual horizon of the world to such an extent as to win for itself an enduring title to the admiration and gratitude of posterity.

The Renaissance in all its vital elements was but an efflorescence of the Middle Ages.

But, in this connection, we should bear in mind that the Renaissance was not a revolution, nor, as its name indicated, a rebirth; but rather the culmination of a centuries-long development during which the Middle Ages advanced beyond the period of infancy and by sheer courage and energy attained the sunlit heights. The society of the Middle Ages after groping for centuries in bold endeavor finally reached and held the summit of progress, rounded the Cape of Good Hope, (1) discovered the New World, invented printing, found anew the buried riches of ancient civilization. There is in this development a social efflorescence of which humanism is but one manifestation. It is the glad budding forth of a sturdy plant, which, before opening to the sunlight and displaying its wealth and excellence, must first experience the wondrous rising of the sap and undergo the patient and hidden work of vegetation.

---

(1) In finally rounding the Cape of Good Hope, after centuries of undaunted efforts, the Portuguese opened the way to India by water. (Tr. n.)

For instance, the route to India was not discovered in a single attempt. A complete account of this great achievement would include the story of the Portuguese navigators, who in hazardous expeditions explored the coasts of Africa from point to point, and thus advanced from one promontory to another. Imagine what an amount of energy, science, adventure was amassed before a man of genius could think of launching out boldly on the unfathomable ocean.

And as to Humanism itself, it was connected with the Middle Ages by an unbroken series of links, from Nicholas V, (1) to Petrarch, (2) from Petrarch to Dante, and from Dante to Charlemagne, without a break in the literary tradition of the classics and without any lagging in the enthusiastic study of these literary masterpieces.

From this aspect, the Renaissance is the continuation of the Middle Ages, the daughter and lawful

(1) Nicolas V., Tomasso Parentucelli, born at Sarzana, Italy, November 15, 1397, was elected Pope February 3, 1337, and died in Rome, March 25, 1455. The aim of his pontificate was to make Rome the home of literature and art, the city of splendid monuments, the worthy capital of the Christian world. During his pontificate scholars of all nations were welcomed to the Vatican as friends, and frequently assisted by him in their financial needs. No department of literature owes him so much as history. The crowning glory of his pontificate was the foundation of the Vatican Library where he sumptuously housed precious manuscripts which his agents had patiently gathered from every country in Europe. (Tr. n.)

(2) Petrarch, Francis, Italian poet and humanist, born July 20, 1304, died July 19, 1374. In 1323 Francis took minor orders and later received a canonical benefice. From 1330 to 1337 he journeyed through France, Germany, and Italy until he finally settled in Vaucluse, France, and there he found the peace and the inspiration that produced so many of his best lyrics. On Easter Sunday, 1341, he was publicly crowned as poet and historian in the Capitol of Rome. As a scholar, Petrarch possessed encyclopedic knowledge much of which he has set down in his various Latin works. His abiding fame is based upon his Italian poetry contained in the "Triumfi" and the "Canzoniere." These begot for Petrarch legions of followers in Italy. Petrarch was the intimate friend of Boccaccio, who, like himself, desired to promote humanistic studies and researches. (Tr. n.)

heiress of the preceding centuries, and not a stranger
who throws upon the marketplace of the European
nations the riches of a newly discovered world.
Doubtless the Renaissance possessed something unknown to the Middle Ages, upholding, as it did, the
pagan conception of life. For some time thereafter
this pagan element prevailed in certain literary centers, but, like an ill chosen graft on a vigorous
trunk, it withered, and undoubtedly it will have no
further influence on the progress of civilization.
The only enduring features of the Renaissance are
the elements which link it to the Catholic and popular tradition of the Middle Ages.

The Middle Ages do not present the ideal state of society.

It will be seen that we are not of the possible
few who believe that the Middle Ages had reached
the ideal perfection of society; nor do we contend
that modern progress is a retrogression to medieval
conditions. No, peoples as well as individuals may
look back in fond recollection to the smiling years of
childhood without longing to be children again. The
Middle Ages are the period of our younger years;
we prize them dearly as the time of our vigorous
youth—a youth not made anemic by lack of light,
not corrupted in a vitiated atmosphere, but a youth
which was freely and proudly developed in the air
and sunlight and which produced the vigorous constitution of our present society. When we pride
ourselves on our present condition, we honor the vigorous red blood of our ancestors.

However, we must admit that our first centuries were not without the defects peculiar to all
childhood. The social temperament of that young
age was marked by an exuberance of spirit and a
lack of discipline which frequently led to violent
outbursts, and its untamed nature asserted itself

even in the most beautiful manifestations of individual and public life. Our fathers were often misled by their imagination, and too often they were victims of an idealism so absolute that at times they seemed to spend their lives in dreams. They lacked confidence in their own power of mind and relied too much on the word of the preceptor; they submitted too readily to teachers who, no doubt, were worthy of respect, but who sometimes were an obstacle to initiative. Moreover, they lacked sufficient experience to appreciate at its full value the civilization they enjoyed; with a naivete almost tragic they were willing to exchange their treasures for the counterfeit money of innovators of all kinds.

These are great defects of which we have partly freed ourselves in the course of centuries, though we may have contracted other defects no less objectionable. Let us repeat that, whatever we are today, we are the outgrowth of the Middle Ages, with their virtues and their faults, drawing our inspiration from the Gospel and not from the Digest, (1) preferring the Magna Charta (2) to the Lex Regia, (3) praying in the Sainte Chapelle (4) rather than in the Parthenon (5). Indeed we may define mod-

---

(1) The term "Digest" is applied in a general sense to the Pandects of Justinian, which are an abridgement, in fifty books, of the decisions, writings, and opinions of the old Roman jurists, made in the sixth century, by direction of the Emperor Justinian, and forming the leading compilation of the Roman civil law. (Tr. n.)

(2) "Magna Charta Libertatis" or the "Great Charter of Liberty," was wrested from King John by the English barons, sustained by Archbishop Stephen Langton on the plains of Runnymede, in 1215. (Tr. n.)

(3) "Lex Regia" or "The Royal Law" was a Roman law relating to the powers of the Roman Emperors. (Tr. n.)

(4) "Sainte Chapelle" is a Catholic church built in Paris, during the reign of St. Louis IX, King of France. in the purest decorated Gothic style. (Tr. n.)

(5) "The Parthenon" was a celebrated pagan temple of Athens. It was built on the Acropolis, of Pentelic marble, in correct Greek style of the Doric variety. (Tr. n.)

ern society to be the society of the Middle Ages at its maturity.

This brings me to my conclusion.

Strictly speaking there are no Middle Ages.

The term "Middle Ages" is but a provisional name which future lexicographers will discard and which in reality designates the youth of the modern world. The golden chain which connects all the Christian centuries has no break, and whatever goes to make up our civilization has its source in the inexhaustible springs of life which were opened up by Christianity nineteen centuries ago. There are no Middle Ages; there is a modern society identically the same from the days of its origin, and this society is the daughter of the Gospel. In this sense, I willingly admit with the English Historian Freeman, (1) that the lines of demarcation drawn by chronologists have but a formal and purely pedagogical value; each period is already contained in the one which precedes it and finds itself again in the one which follows.

The Line of Demarcation in the world's history is Golgotha.

But I hasten to add that to this rule there is a transcendent and unique exception. There is a line of demarcation which separates into two grand divisions the history of humankind. It is the line which bears on its summit the Cross of Golgotha. And why? Because it is there that was heard the Fiat Lux (Light be made) of a second creation; because thence there came down upon the world the new law of a new civilization, the New Commandment as Christ Himself called it. On the day when it was said to the individual: "Love God above all

---

(1)   Freeman, "The Methods of Historical Study."

things and thy neighbor as thyself for the love of God"; to the citizen: "Render to God the things that are God's and to Caesar the things that are Caesar's"; to the State: "Seek first the kingdom of God and its justice" (1)—on that day there arose a new morality, a new public law, a new social ideal. Like a mysterious leaven, the creative word worked upon and permeated humanity, and all the manifestations of justice and love there produced from century to century are but the result of this marvelous fermentation: "The kingdom of heaven is like to leaven, which a woman took and hid in three measures of meal, until the whole was leavened". (2)

On the day when the Christian religion gave to mankind its compass and pointed out its polar star, there began for humanity a life worth living, a life of which the ancient poet (3) seemed to have had an obscure presentiment when on the frontispiece of the new world he wrote this grand verse:

Magnus ab integro saeculorum nascitur ordo.

The great order of ages is born anew.

Then, walking under the shadow of the cross, the Christian centuries took the road of the future.

Vexilla Regis prodeunt.

Crucis fulget mysterium (4).

The royal banners now unfurled,

The mystic cross illumines the world.

From its birth Christian society has marched on

---

(1)   Matthew VI, 33.
(2)   St. Matthew XIII, 33.
(3)   The ancient poet here quoted is Virgil. He was born 70 B. C. He is the author of the "Eclogues" (pastoral poems), the "Georgics" (rural poems), and the "Aeneid," the greatest epic poem in the Latin language. The diffusion of the Messianic prophecies throughout the nations had made the world look for a Savior of mankind and a consequent new and brighter era of history. Virgil gave expression to this universal expectancy in the sublime verse quoted. (Tr. n.)
(4)   Opening lines of the Vespers hymn during the Passiontide.   (Tr. n.)

its checkered course towards the realization of its
sublime ideal. The centuries of the Middle Ages
began the work; the modern centuries followed; and
our age, heir of both, continues the task and will
hand down the work unfinished to future centuries.

Vicissitudes and future of Christian Civilization.

The edifice of Christian civilization is not unlike those grand Gothic cathedrals the inspired architects of which could but draw the plans and lay the
foundations without seeing their idea realized here
below. Generation after generation came to the foot
of the edifice and continued the labor of love. They
lavished upon it all their talent and wealth; at times
they matched the genius of the inspired master; at
other times in their enthusiasm they hid the leading
architectural lines under a profusion of flowers;
then again, by the barrenness or the exuberance of
their work, they sometimes put into jeopardy the
very principles of Christian art. Thus the venerable
monument bears the imprint of all the passing pre-
dilections of art. Nay more, in this prolonged work
of generations there were times when the hand grew
weary, when courage drooped, when the building
material slept at the foot of the edifice. This was
so true of the Cathedral of Cologne as to give rise to
the legend that the structure would never be finished, that the devil would not permit it. . . . Nevertheless, in spite of the devil and his imps, the Cathedral of Cologne has been finished and the twin
crosses of its spires glisten in the blue of heaven.

As with the noble Temple of Cologne, so with
the edifice of Catholic civilization. Divers hands
and opposite talents have worked towards its com-
pletion, times of inaction with their train of gloomy
tales have befallen it, but to-day new legions of

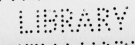

workers swarm about its sides as they spend themselves in the work of raising the sacred spires to
loftier and still loftier heights.

APPENDIX

Medieval archeology during the seventeenth century.

The ignorance of men of the seventeenth and eighteenth
centuries concerning the history of medieval art is simply
appalling. They could not even see the difference between
the Romanesque and Gothic styles for both of which they
expressed equal contempt. Thus, for instance, in 1686, the
celebrated Gilbert Burnett, Anglican archbishop of Salisbury,
writes as follows concerning the beautiful Romanesque cathedral of Worms: "There is little remarkable in the cathedral, which is a huge building in the Gothic manner of the
worst sort." The archeological science of the time recognized
two kinds of Gothic: "The ancient, originating with the
Goths in the fifth century (massive, heavy and coarse buildings), and the modern buildings more delicate, lighter and
surprisingly bold."

Such texts should be put in parallel columns with the
celebrated verses of the "Art Poetique" of Boileau on the
poetry and the theatre of the Middle Ages; they constitute,
so to say, documents of the first rank for "the intellectual
history" of the modern epoch and they account in a way for
the vandalism which was rampant during the eighteenth century and during the first half of the nineteenth century.

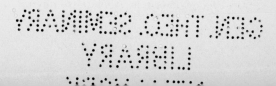